THE GERMANS IN TEXAS

A STUDY IN IMMIGRATION

By
GILBERT GIDDINGS BENJAMIN, PH. D.,
Sometime Fellow and Assistant in History in Yale University; Instructor in History in the College of the City of New York.

PHILADELPHIA
(Reprinted from German American Annals, Vol. VII.)
1909

Notice

In many older books, foxing (or discoloration) occurs and, in some instances, print lightens with wear and age. Reprinted books, such as this, often duplicate these flaws, notwithstanding efforts to reduce or eliminate them. The pages of this reprint have been digitally enhanced and, where possible, the flaws eliminated in order to provide clarity of content and a pleasant reading experience.

Copyright © 1910 by Gilbert Giddings Benjamin.

First Published :
Philadelphia
1909

Reprinted by:

Janaway Publishing, Inc.
732 Kelsey Ct.
Santa Maria, California 93454
(805) 925-1038
www.janawaygenealogy.com

2010

ISBN 10: 1596412119
ISBN 13: 9781596412118

Made in the United States of America

THIS WORK IS AFFECTIONATELY INSCRIBED TO

PROFESSOR ANDREW WHEELER PHILLIPS,

DEAN OF THE GRADUATE SCHOOL,

YALE UNIVERSITY,

MENTOR AND FRIEND.

TABLE OF CONTENTS.

CHAPTER I.

	Pages
German Immigration From 1815 to 1848............	1–9

CHAPTER II.

Early German Settlements With Reasons for Settlement — 10–24

CHAPTER III.

The Society of German Princes and Nobles Formed for the Purpose of Aiding Germans to Settle in Texas. Its Aims. Its Influence on German Immigration.. — 25–54

CHAPTER IV.

Numbers of Germans in Texas. Industries. Cotton Culture. Wages. Character and Method of Life. Comparison and Relations With the Americans... — 55–89

CHAPTER V.

Slavery. Number of Negroes in the German Settlements. Attitude of Germans Toward Slavery, Secession and Reconstruction.................. — 90–110

CHAPTER VI.

Elements of Culture. Schools. Newspapers. Singing Societies and Societies for Intellectual Improvement. Literature. Religion. Examples of Cultured Germans .... — 111–126

CHAPTER VII.

Relations With the Indians. Brief Account of the Smaller German Settlements................... — 127–133
Bibliography .... — 133–139
Appendices . ... — 139–155
Maps .... — 157–161

GERMANS IN TEXAS.

CHAPTER I.
German Immigration From 1815 to 1848.

In a recent work[1] Gonnard states that "considered in its entirety, during the fifty years from 1840-1890, German immigration is an epoch. From year to year with the regularity of a physical phenomenon, a regularity greater than the majority of physical phenomena, there scattered over the new World and certain parts of the Old, without speaking of the countries adjacent to Europe, some hundred millions of men". Although this is not true for the preceding half century, the immigration was amazingly great in comparison with earlier periods. To quote the same author further: "There was a moment in the history of the 19th century when it could be asked, whether the United States would be Anglo-Saxon or German, at least in certain of its parts. The Teutonic immigration has indeed fallen upon this country with a force and continuity almost incomparable."[2] A further investigation will show that this statement is not an exaggeration during the period under discussion. From 1832 to 1846, from Bremen, a hundred thousand Germans, to put it in round numbers, immigrated to America, or on the average 11,000 yearly. From 1841 to 1846, the yearly average of German immigrants amounted to 19,000. According to statistics made by Franz Löher in 1847, the following is the exact yearly number of immigrants from 1841 to 1846:—[3]

```
1841—  9,501
1842— 13,627
1843—  9,910
1844— 19,641
1845— 31,358
1846— 31,607
```

Total—115,644

---

[1] Gonnard, *L'Emigration Européene au XIX Siècle*, Paris, 1906, p. 110.
[2] Ibid, p. 145ff.
[3] Löher, Franz, *Geschichte und Züstande der Deutschen in America*. Cincinnati and Leipzig, 1847, p. 271.

In fifteen years, a grand total of 216,201 Germans immigrated to this country from Bremen alone. The following is a table for the same years of the number of emigrants departing from Bremen and landing at the ports named:—[4]

To New York, 33,683 and in the year 1846 alone 10,469
" Baltimore, 30,123   "   "   "   8,470
" New Orleans, 30,448 "   "   "   7,690
" Philadelphia, 3,580 "   "   "   938
" Charleston, 728   "   "   "   116
" Galveston, 7,161   "   "   "   3,338
" Quebec, 426   "   "   "   420

For the year 1847 the same authority shows the following numbers:—

New York—52,300
New Orleans—20,000
Baltimore—10,000
Galveston—8,000. Landed here, in the last three months (previous to July, 1847) 4,020 Germans.
Philadelphia—5,000.
Quebec—1,000.
Boston—500. (15,504 emigrants landed here up to Dec. 1, 1846.)
Mobile, Savannah and other harbors—1,000.

Some 600,000 Germans landed in America in the fifteen years previous to 1847 from the various ports of departure, or on the average, about 40,000 Germans annually. The chief point of departure for the Southern Germans was Havre. Bremen was the principal port taken by the Eastern and Northern Germans.[5]

That this great stream of immigration did not remain unrecognized in the United States is shown by the following:

"The emigration from Europe in the present season appears much greater than ever it was before. It already much exceeds 100,000 persons, say 50,000 or more via Quebec and the remainder

---

[4] Ibid, p. 272.
[5] Löher, Franz, *Geschichte und Züstande der Deutschen in America.* Cincinnati and Leipzig, 1847, p. 271.

by way of New York, Philadelphia, Baltimore, etc. At the last named places, and especially Baltimore, very many Germans have arrived." [6]

"We learn that the increasing prospect of internal commotion in the German Empire is the main cause of this immigration. * * * We are further informed by some of the most intelligent that it is calculated not less than 80,000 are now moving and preparing to depart for this country." [7]

We may well ask ourselves the question how came this tremendous mass of immigrants and what was its character.

The causes which impelled this tide of immigration are many and complex. The Napoleonic wars as a matter of course devastated a great portion of the land, and drove many from employment. The business depression from 1815 on caused great distress.[8] The reactionary movement of Metternich and his confrères resulted in almost universal dissatisfaction. The "Deutsche Burschenschaft" was the chief means of arousing a spirit of discontent in Germany.[9] Its declared objects were the fostering of high moral ideals, of patriotism and a truly scientific spirit. Some of its members had definite political ideas. Some believed in a German republic; others wanted to restore the empire. The Kotzebue incident brought affairs to a crisis. At a conference of the representatives of the two great powers, Austria and Prussia, held in Carlsbad, a reactionary movement was agreed upon. A severe censorship of the press was established and a special commission was appointed to investigate "demagogical intrigues." For ten years, this commission persecuted everyone suspected of liberal ideas.

The revolution of July, 1830, in Paris was followed by revolts in the Rhenish Palatinate in May, 1832, and in Frankfurt and in Oberhessen in 1833. The immediate cause of these uprisings was the so-called "Bundestags Ordonnanzen" of the year 1831.

---

[6] Cf. *Niles Weekly Register*, Sept., 1832; March, 1833. Vol. XLIII or Vol. VII, Fourth Series, p. 40.

[7] Cf. *The York*, [Pa.] *Republican* quoted in *Niles Register*, Vol. VII, Fourth Series, p. 68.

[8] Cf. *Deutsche Pionier*, Vol. I, p. 243ff. "The Three Periods of German Immigration."

[9] See Bruncken, *German Political Refugees from 1815-1860*. Ch. 3, 1904.

The time was ripe for emigration. America had always appeared to the oppressed and discontented as the home of liberty, of freedom of speech and of the press. The use of the word "Europamüde" at this time shows the feeling then prevalent, and implies that there was a land free from oppression. Many of the discontented left home. Some settled in nearby countries, but the younger spirits sought the United States as a place where their political ideas might take root and thrive. Those who left sent letters home. These were passed from hand to hand. The newspapers were filled with accounts either by immigrants or regarding immigration. At this time many books of travel were published. Those of Arends, Eggerling, Brauns, Bromme, Gerke and Duden were the most important. The work[10] of Duden had a far-reaching influence. It first appeared in 1829, and went through several editions.

---

[10] Its title reads: *Bericht über eine Reise nach den westlichen Staaten Nord Amerika's und einen mehrjährigen Aufenthalt am Missouri (in den Jahren, 1824, 1825, 1826 und 1827) in Bezug auf Auswanderung und Uebervölkerung oder Das Leben im Innern der Vereinigten Staaten und dessen Bedeutung für die häusliche und politische Lage der Europäer, dargestellt: a, in einer Sammlung von Briefen; b, in einer Abhandlung über den politischen Zustand der Nord Amerikaner; c, in einem Nachtrage für auswandernde Deutsche Ackerwirthe und diejenigen welche auf Handelsunternehmungen denken von Gottfried Duden, St. Gallen, 1832.*

The preface of the 1832 edition reads as follows:

"Von Tag zu Tag gewinnt das Land des Colombo, Amerika, an Bedeutung, auch für uns. Die Uebervölkerung Europas wird endlich obwohl spät, auch von unsern Statistikern als dessen Ruin angesehen, dem es, starken Laufes, zueilt. Die Armuth, der Druck jeglicher Art, die volksausdörrenden Finanzsysteme, die Bemauthung bilden bei uns, unsichtbar und um desto gefährlicher, eine Art Leibeigenschaft für die gemeinen Volsksklassen der gewerbtreibenden Staaten, welche die eigentliche gesetzliche Sklaverei unläugbar in Vielen überbietet. Dazu kommt dass sich dem Kennen von Geschichte und Politik immer umwiderleglicher aufdringt: die Sonnen Europas haben ihren Mittagskreis längst überschritten, und dessen Geschichte, dessen Völker—ihre Rolle ausgespieldt. Wie das Licht, das der Sonne, wie das der Bildung und Kultur, im Osten, in Asien, für uns anbrach, und bei uns untergeht, um für die westliche Halbkugel Morgen zu schaffen, so beginnt in Amerika seit einem halben Jahrhundert eine neue Weltgeschichte, und wir können es nicht läugnen, die der Freiheit, der grossen Ideen. Amerika ist für den Forscher eine Brücke vom Nord-zum Südpol, auf der sich die letzten Trümmer morgenländischer Bildung zu einem neuen, grossen Baue retten und sammeln werden. Die politischen Ereignisse in Deutschland, und die Wendung, die das Streben der Völker nach Emanzipation letzter Tage genommen zu haben scheint, werden diese, wenn auch des Europäers Seele mit Wehmuth belastende Ansicht, kaum zu widerlegen im Stande sein. Die kindische Idee hat aufgehört, dass man in Amerika sogleich am Strande die Taschen mit Gold füllen könne; aber Eines verheisst es dem besonnen

Duden visited this country in 1824. He landed at Baltimore and went to Missouri. At that time few Europeans had ever heard of that river. After a stay of three years in this country, he returned and published his book in the form of letters. These were written in a lively style and gave a very rosy picture of life in the Western World. It resulted in thousands of men dreaming of western adventure and settlement.[11] He[12] gives wonderful descriptions of the fertility of the soil, the personal liberty of the settler, and the great abundance of game of all kinds. He declares that one can live with hardly any labor of his hands. His influence was particularly strong in Southwest Germany and along the Rhine. It is very noticeable that most of the immigrants of political tendencies came from these regions.

Now an entirely different kind of emigration to America set in. The former emigration was mainly incited by economic reasons, the new emigration was influenced by political and romantic ideas. Duden's radical tendencies were entirely in accord with these views. The stream of emigration was made up of educated men and those of the better class. This political emigration came in more or less organized groups. They had more or less definite ideas of establishing States in the United States. These States might or might not be members of the Union.[13] They were to be predominantly German in character. German was to be the language of business, school and government. German culture should flourish unhindered. Some of the bolder spirits even went further in their ideas. "They would have the Government of the United States itself bi-lingual, and if the Americans would not grant this—why, then the German States would secede and set up a national government of their own"[14]

Auswanderer umstreitig; hohe Freiheit und Sicherung leiblichen Wohlstandes in einem Grade, von dem Europa keine Ahnung hat. Millionen finden in den herrlichen Ebenen und Thälern des Missouri und Mississippi Raum vollauf, und eine Natur die längst des Bewohners, des Bearbeiters harret."
"Herausgeber."

[11] For Duden's influence cf. *Duetsche Pionier*, Vol. I, p. 18.

[12] See Bruncken, *Ger. Pol. Refugees*, p. 16, and Baker, *Young Germany in America*, p. 50. (Reprint from *Americana Germanica*.)

[13] For fuller accounts regarding these ideas cf. Baker, *Young Germany*, p. 61ff.; also Bruncken, Ch. 2.

[14] Bruncken, Ch. 3.

Societies were formed to bring these plans to maturity. The most important was the "Giessener Auswanderungs-Gesellschaft."[15] It was organized originally by a number of university men, among whom Paul Follen was the leading spirit. Its aims as stated in a pamphlet issued in 1833[16] were: "The founding of a German state, which would, of course, have to be a member of the United States, but with maintenance of a form of government which will assure the continuance of German custom, German language, and create genuine, free and popular life." The intention was to occupy an unsettled and unorganized territory "in order that a German republic, a rejuvenated Germany may arise in North America." The members were men of means. Some held high official and professional positions. They sailed from Bremen to New Orleans in 1834 in two vessels. After their arrival in this country, dissensions arose and the company was broken up. Paul Follen settled in Missouri on Duden's farm and lived there several years. An account of such an undertaking is given in Niles' Register and shows clearly what vague ideas were prevalent at this time.[17]

Many similar societies were formed with this plan in view. The idea was not only taken up in Germany, but found followers among the Germans in this country. In Philadelphia in 1836,

---

[15] Cf. Bruncken, Ch. 3; Baker, p. 61ff.; Koerner, *Das deutsche Element*, p. 300ff.

[16] Cf. *Aufforderung und Erklärung in Betreff einer Auswanderung im Grossen aus Deutschland in die nordamerikanischen Freistaaten*. Giessen, 1883. See *Der deutsche Pionier*, Vol. I. p. 18.

[17] Vol. VII, Fourth Series, p. 148. "Wholesale Emigration." The *Stuttgart Universal Gazette* of September 2d announces that a plan is in progress in the southwest of Germany, to make up a state and ship it over to the United States to become a twenty-fifth member of the Confederacy. The following notice of the project appears in that publication: "According to accounts from the South-West of Germany a society of liberal men are organizing a grand plan for emigrating to North America.

"The emigration has hitherto been precarious because it did not rest on any solid foundation and because the means were not concentrated. But now it is different, as the object is to form a *New Germany* beyond the ocean, which is to receive all those whose hopes and claims to liberty and right are disappointed in old Germany. In order to be admitted into the confederation of the United States, the law requires the number of free inhabitants above 25 years of age to be 60,000, and this number is to be assembled before any further measures can be taken. Many of the Germans established in North America will join their countrymen and the plan is so popular, that scarcely any doubts are entertained of its being successful."

a society was formed with the purposes of founding a German State in the United States. Its object was announced as "The unification of the Germans in North America and by this means the founding of a new German Fatherland."

In New York, in 1839, a society for the purpose of colonizing Texas was formed. This was the "Germania Gesellschaft." It sent out on the 2d of November, of that year 130 persons to form a German State in the "Lone Star Republic." The emigrants departed on the brig "North" which was owned by the society. The members had pledged themselves to cultivate a piece of land in common for a period of three years. After this period, it was to be divided among the members. The members consisted of men of all classes and stations in life. Provisions for a period of six or eight months had been provided, together with all kinds of implements for the construction of houses. At Galveston, a station was to be erected, to which the arrivals of the second division might resort. The first colonists reached Texas without any misfortunes and landed at Houston. The president and those who had any money left returned to New York. The majority of the others came to want.[18]

In the year 1841, the Teutonia Order was formed in Texas. Its existence was brief. Fritz Ernst, who settled in Texas in the early thirties, published an account of the order. He says:

"It remains for them (the Germans) either to become entirely changed, so as to come to be called Americans * * * or to make the attempt in a social way among the few Germans living here to form a New Germany. * * * The former appears to us, as certainly to all feeling Germans, as entirely impossible and must remain committed to our successors; and the latter can only be practicable, if all countrymen be united collectively through a bond; if concord, which only too easily disappears in a foreign land, be established among them, and their feeling for German individuality be renewed, and their consciousness of their German worth be incited.

"Since the population of Texas consists of immigrants from different countries, who must all consider themselves here as foreigners, this plan appears in Texas more easily to be carried out, than in the North American free states where a generation born there has been formed as the leading race."

---

[18] Büttner, *Briefe*, Vol. II, p. 209; also Eickhoff, *In der neuen Heimath*, pp. 324-325.

"Many men and women gathered together as a result of the attempt to carry out this national work, who took up the idea with enthusiasm, and after mature consideration formed a Teutonic order which was established on the evening of Whitsuntide, 1841, by twelve persons of both sexes and whose personnel through later admissions of members amounted in the course of a month to fifty-three, and increased with each meeting. The order was made up of many degrees, so that less educated Germans might take part. Admission to the second and third degrees was conditioned on talent and ability; all the Germans living away from home must be received into membership, because it guarantees intellectual entertainment, profit and pleasure to compensate in some measure for the lost joys of the Fatherland, and because it embraces in itself the elements of various secret and knightly orders, and thereby breathes pure German nationality. Among its manifold aims the most important are: philanthropy and the preservation of German individual traits of character."[19] Körner[20] gives the purpose of the order as: 'The preservation of German national individuality, the furtherance of German immigration and the facilitation of correspondence between Texas and Germany.'"

In this connection, brief mention must be made of the so-called "Adelsverein", as its aims were undoubtedly the same as the others noted. Von Behr says: "It is said the Union wished to found a feudal state, which would lend money to its settlers and they would be treated in a way as its own property."[21] We shall treat this society more fully in a later chapter.

What was the character of the immigration of this period? Grund, in his work published in 1837, says:

"Until recently the emigrants from Germany were chiefly composed of agriculturists, with an occasional admixture of operatives, but the late unfortunate struggle for liberty in Germany has, within the last five or six years, caused the expatriation of a more intelligent class; and, accordingly, settlements have been made in the valley of the Mississippi and in the State of Illinois, by a body of Germans whose education fitted them rather for the drawing-room and the closet than for the hardships of cultivating the soil; yet they have cheerfully embraced their new vocation; and the physicians, lawyers, theological and other students who arrived about three

---

[19] Cf. *Deutsche-Amerikanische Geschichtsblätter*, Jan., 1906, pp. 21-22.
[20] "Erhaltung der deutschen National-Eigenthümlichkeit. Beförderung der deutschen Einwanderung und Erleichterung der Korrespondenz zwischen Texas und Deutschlands." Körner, p. 359.
[21] Von Behr, Ottomar, Leipzig, 1847.

years ago in the United States have become active husbandmen; though they were obliged to resign the romantic idea of founding a new Germany in the western territory of the United States,"[22] and *Niles Register* says that "the mania for emigration to America, as it is called, increases—and many persons of wealth were preparing to leave different parts of Germany." [23]

These quotations will suffice to show that the emigration during this period was made up of a class different from that of the earlier period. Men of wealth, position and education emigrated to America in great numbers. Many among them had held high official or professional positions at home. The "Forty-eighters" swelled the ranks of this class of immigrants.

---

[22] Cf. Grund, F. J.: *The Americans.* London, 1837. Vol. II, pp. 24-25.
[23] Cf. *Niles Weekly Register,* Vol. XLIII, p. 149.

CHAPTER II.

EARLY GERMAN SETTLERS WITH REASONS FOR SETTLEMENT.

It is an interesting commentary that no history yet written of Texas contains any extended mention of the Germans in that State. It is interesting from several viewpoints. In that State an attempt was made to further on a large scale, immigration such as probably no other State has known. The Germans have formed a most important part of its population from the very beginning; Germans took part in the Texan War of Independence, and one of the most interesting accounts of that war was written by a German who was a participant personally in many of its engagements; the Germans as a class were educated and cultured, many of them belonging to high rank in their own country and many were possessed of means; under their auspices the first public school supported by taxation was established; many of the officials of the State have been Germans; and one, Gustave Schleicher, had already gained a national reputation before his death and was destined to still higher honors had he lived, according to James A. Garfield and former Secretary of State Bayard.

In 1846 the laws of Texas were ordered to be translated into German.[1] That they had early gained an important influence is shown by the fact that as early as 1843 the Texan Congress granted the right of incorporating a university to certain Germans who were residents of the "Lone Star Republic." For this purpose a league of land was donated by the Congress.[2]

The accounts regarding these Germans, as far as Texas is concerned, are meagre, and are to be found only in brief articles in journals or in books dealing with memoirs of pioneers. It is strange that no account has yet been written of a people, who, as early as 1847, formed one-fifth of the white population. Their

---

[1] *Fest Ausgabe zum fünfzigjährigen Jubiläum*, 1906. Foot note, p. 86. Tait's *Edinburgh Magazine*, 1848, p. 224. *Allgemeine Zeitung*, No. 62, Mar. 3, 1847.

[2] Cf. *Laws of Eighth Congress of Texas*, p. 948ff.

attitude toward slavery and their competition with slave labor would seem to have deserved some mention. Perhaps the future historian of the State will give them their due regard.

Even before Texas had gained its independence, many German families were found in that territory. The reasons why they came there and their experiences are most romantic.

In 1818-19, a German traveller visited Texas. Texas, at that time, still belonged to Spain. He published a work on his travels in the United States, in which he makes special mention of Texas. It is interesting to speculate what might have happened had his ideas been carried out. The Monroe Doctrine had not yet been promulgated. A German state on this side of the water might have been no impossibility, as it was certain to have been at a later period. His book must certainly have had readers, and doubtless it may have fallen into the hands of some of the early German settlers in this territory. He describes the country as extraordinarily fruitful in wheat, maize, cotton and indigo; the climate in the interior, on account of the many mountains, is healthful and temperate; only on the coast are there any swamps.[3] He was a lieutenant in the Prussian army, and suggested the colonization of Texas by Prussia. He says that there are lead mines[4] in the province at present being worked. Says that the country produces not only tropical, but all European vegetables; that grapes are grown and wine is being produced; that 800 pounds of cotton can be grown to the acre; that the voyage to Texas can be made in eight or nine weeks with favorable winds. He describes the condition of Spanish agriculture as extremely poor. San Antonio was the chief city, with about 2,000 inhabitants, most of them living in a wretched condition. The cities of the province of Texas number about 12,000 persons. He advises Prussian colonization[5] in the following words:

"If there is a piece of land on the transatlantic continent favorable to a colonial possession for Prussia, it is the province of Texas whose acquisition by purchase from Spain, to whom it has neither

[3] Hecke, J. V., *Reise durch die Vereinigten Staaten*, 1818-1819. Berlin, 1821. Vol. I, p. 195ff.
[4] *Ibid.* Vol. II, pp. 170-189.
[5] *Ibid.* Vol. I, p. 195ff.

use nor political advantage, might be very easily made. Certainly very important results in agricultural, political and mercantile respects, would accrue from the possession of a stretch of land which is greater than Germany. Although at present there is no, or very little, civilized population; in a short time it would become a flourishing colony, if Prussia would make use of the emigrants from Germany, who, having become beggars through the voyage, suffer wretchedly in the United States; furnish them free transportation on Prussian ships; give them the land either gratuitously or grant them support, if only by advanced payments; then they would have cultivated after five, or at the most, ten years, fifty acres (Morgen) of fertile land. If one reckons only a frugal revenue from the soil as thirty grain, then the colonist, after reserving a third part of his ground for the cultivation of fodder and vegetables, receiving from the remaining thirty-two acres nine hundred and sixty bushels of wheat, reckoning this at one and a half Thaler per bushel, will receive a pure revenue of 1,440 Thaler yearly and be able to pay back all sums advanced to him with good interest."

He continues by stating that the mountains in the interior of the country have never been investigated; that rich metallurgical finds may be expected. He would use criminals to work these mines and would transport for that purpose all that have in any way broken the law.

To quote further:

"The advantages in a commercial respect would be not less important for the mother country, in that (a) all commerce with the Indians as far as the Pacific Ocean would come into the hands of the Prussians; (b) for Prussian manufacturing, Galveston Bay would be a very suitable emporium, in order that from there trade might be carried on along the Rio del Norte into Mexico, and on the Mississippi, the Missouri, Ohio, Sabine and Red Rivers into the United States.

"Through such commercial canals, Prussia would receive the tropical products at first hand, or it could raise cotton, indigo and sugar itself, and this circumstance would have a very important influence on the condition of manufacturing.

"The sum for which this acquisition could be obtained would not be very heavy, and in case the government would not desire to furnish or to spare the necessary amount, the merchants, who would receive most of the advantage from this colonial possession, might, without difficulty, advance payments to the State; but, as soon as Spain has shown itself ready to grant the cession, a commercial company might be formed like the East India Company, which should defray all expenses, but also should derive all profits, and the State must only furnish the requisite troops for the protection of the colony. Prussian trade would receive through such a possession, a wholly different expansion, life and spirit within ten years, and perhaps after this time, in case the colony, as already agreed upon, should form a suitable constitution, it would number a million inhabitants. And by no means the least to be reckoned are the advantages which would result immediately to Prussia from the possession of such a piece of land."

He continues by saying that Prussia could send over 10,000 invalid soldiers in order to protect the colony. These could be given possession of land as a gift. With these, the colonists could form a militia to prevent danger from any invasion.

Prussia's navy would be built up through this colonial possession. "Only through navigation and sea trade can an industrious nation gain wealth." Only by means of its navy has England reached its present position. "Only through its navy has colossal Russia risen so high in commercial industries, in wealth, and in culture of the spirit that it is the marvel and wonder of the age."

"This colony would furnish with grain, salt flesh, butter and other products, not only the archipelago of the Antilles, but also the entire northern and eastern coast of the South American continent with the exception of Brazil."

Whether the publication of this work had any influence or not, many settlements of Germans were located in Texas in the early thirties. Before these settlers had appeared, a company of fifty-three adventurers landed on the Texan coast. They came from New Orleans in October, 1821. They marched to Goliad (La Bohia) and took possession of it. They were made prisoners by Mexican soldiers. In the State archives there is a report which gives their names and nationalities. Among those mentioned, the following Germans are found: Eduard Hanstein, Joseph Dirksen, Ernst von Rosenberg, Wilhelm Miller, Carl Cuans, and Gasper Porton.[6] Ernst von Rosenberg joined the Mexican army in whose service he rose to the rank of colonel of artillery. He took the side of Iturbide and was shot upon the downfall of the latter. It has been stated that the so-called

---

[6] Rosenberg, *Kritik*, p. 6. Brown, *Indian Wars and Pioneers of Texas*, p. 283.

"Baron de Bastrop," who aided Austin in his colonization schemes, without whose intervention Anglo-American colonization would have utterly failed, was a German.[7] It has been shown from official documents that he had a Spanish name.[8] Much has been written about his colonizing of Germans in Texas. Roemer,[9] in his work, states in discussing a visit he made to the town of Bastrop that the "city is called after a certain Baron v. Bastrop, who had in view an important German colonization undertaking, and had already obtained an important piece of land." His plans were later prevented on account of his death. Koerner[10] states that the colony of Bastrop was settled by Oldenburgians from the Duchy of Delmenhorst. Mr. H. A. Ratterman, the editor of the *Deutsche Pionier,* says that in 1823 Bastrop brought a number of Oldenburgian peasants and founded the city of Bastrop.[11]

Whatever the truth may be regarding Bastrop's having settled Germans in Texas in the twenties, already in the early thirties several flourishing settlements are found.

Two Germans are mentioned among the early Mexican impressarios to receive grants under the colonization law of Mexico. These were Joseph Vehlein and Robert Lestwich. The former held a half of the original Hayden Edward grant between the Sabine and the Navasoto; the latter had a contract to bring in two hundred families.[12] Among the first real German settlers, however, was a Friedrich Ernst. He was a bookkeeper[13] and emigrated from Barel, Duchy of Oldenburg.[14] In 1829, Ernst

---

[7] Cf. Rather: *DeWitt Colony,* Texas Historical Association Quarterly, 1904-5, p. 98.

[8] Letter from E. W. Winkler, Department of Agriculture, Insurance Statistics and History, Austin, Texas, of this year (1907).

[9] Roemer, F., *Texas,* p. 208.

[10] Koerner, *Das deutsche Element,* p. 359.

[11] *Deutsche Pionier,* Vol. 16, No. 9, p. 372. The same author in *Deutsch-Amerikanisches Magazin,* 1886, p. 402, says under the heading, "Die Ansiedlungs-Projekte des Barons Bastrop," that Bastrop had many colonization plans; that the City of Bastrop was laid out in 1823, and that he bases his statement on Ehrenberg.

[12] Schem, *Conversations Lexicon,* Vol. X, pp. 691ff.

[13] Biography of Fordtran says that Ernst was a gardner. Cf. Brown, *Indian Wars and Pioneers,* p. 424ff.

[14] "*Life of German Pioneers in Early Texas.*" Cf. Texas Historical Quarterly, Vol. II, p. 227ff. Article by Caroline von Hinueber, daughter of Ernst.

decided to go to America. He came to New York and bought a hotel.[15] Duden's book came into his hands and he determined to settle in Missouri. This was in the year 1831. While in New York he met Charles Fordtran. They set sail for New Orleans. While in that city, they learned that every settler with his family would receive a league and labor[16] of land from the Mexican Government,[17] so they decided upon immigrating to Texas. They set sail in the Mexican schooner "Saltillo," and landed at Harrisburgh, in April, 1831. They remained in that place some five weeks, while Fordtran went ahead and entered a league of land where the town of Industry now stands. They travelled on oxcarts to San Felipe de Austin which had some three to four hundred inhabitants. Ernst is evidently the first German to bring his family into Texas. At that time there were a few unmarried Germans in Texas.[18] They had no neighbors as far north as the White River, in Arkansas, and east to the Sabine River, and south to the settlement at San Felipe. They had only one neighbor to the west. It was twenty-eight miles to San Felipe. It is interesting to note the hardships endured by those early settlers. The house was a hut covered with straw, and having six sides made of moss.[19] Mrs. Ernst slept without a pillow, on a deer skin on the floor. At first they had only corn bread to eat, and later only cow peas. The nearest mill was thirty miles distant.

Ernst wrote to his former neighbors. This letter was published in the local newspaper. Through this means a number of Oldenburgers and Münsterländers with their families were brought to Texas in 1834.[20] Among them were the families of

---

[15] *Deutsche Pionier*, Vol. 16, No. 9, p. 3ff.

[16] League was 4428.4 acres; a labor was 177, or one-twenty-fifth of a league or sitio.

[17] According to account of Mrs. Hinueber quoted above. In Fordtran's biography, it is stated that they met an American on their way to New Orleans while on board the steamer, and he influenced them to go to Texas. See Brown, p. 424ff.

[18] Mrs. Hineuber mentions a Hertzner, a tailor, and a Grossmeyer—*Deutsche Pionier* calls the name Wertzner.

[19] The *Civilian and Galveston Gazette*, Dec. 2, 1843, mentions a settler who came in the thirties, evidently Ernst. It says that he built a camp interwoven between the angles with moss.

[20] *Der Deutsche Pionier*, article by Mrs. Ernst, says that through Fordtran's efforts some German immigrants were brought to Texas. Cf. above.

Bartels, Zimmerschreib, Iurgens, Ainsler, Walters, Kleberg, von Roedel, Siebel and Grasmeyer. Robert Kleberg, Sr., in his memoir mentions the names R. D. Stolje (probably Stoelke) and wife, Reinerman and wife, Bartels, Damke, William Vrels, John Hemike and George Herder. Ernst became an influential man in the republic. He took part in the Texan Revolution, and was one of the members of "the Teutonia Order," and one of the incorporators of Hermann University. Fordtran received a contract to bring in eight hundred families.

Through a letter sent by Ernst to his home in the Duchy of Oldenburg, a number of Germans were brought to Texas. Among these were the families von Roeder and Kleberg. It does not seem fitting in an account of the early Germans in Texas to omit some mention of Robert Justus Kleberg, Sr. He was born in Herstelle, Westphalia, and graduated doctor juris from Göttingen. In 1834, he determined to emigrate. In an account[21] written about him, he is said to have said:

"I wished to live under a republican form of government, with unbounded personal, religious and political liberty, free from the petty tyrannies, the many disadvantages and evils of old countries. I was an enthusiastic lover of liberty, and I expected to find in Texas, above all countries, the blessed land of my most fervent hopes."

How he happened to choose Texas for his home is told in a memoir which he kept. He says:

"We had accidentally got hold of a letter written by a gentleman, who had emigrated some time before us from the Duchy of Oldenburg and who lived near where now is Industry, Texas, Fritz Ernst by name. In this letter he had described Texas, then a province of Mexico, in very glowing colors, mentioning also, the advantages offered by the Mexican government, namely, a league and a labor for every man with a family and one-half league for every single man. This letter caused us to change our first intentions to go to one of the northern States and to choose Texas for our future home. At the time we left, hardly anything was known of Texas, except that my ideas and those of my party were formed by the above mentioned letter, in which Texas was described as a beautiful country, with enchanting scenery and delightful climate, similar to that of Italy, the most fruitful soil and republican government with unbounded personal and political liberty, free from so many dis-

---

[21] Brown, *Indian Wars and Pioneers of Texas*, p. 289.

advantages and evils of old countries. Prussia, our former home, smarted at the time we left, under a military despotism. We were enthusiastic lovers of republican institutions, full of romantic notions, and believed to find in Texas, before all other countries, the blessed land of our hope."[22]

This memoir shows what induced men of his stamp to leave the Fatherland, and is incidentally interesting, as it gives an idea how the immigrants to the new land influenced others to follow. The company of which Kleberg was a member was made up of himself and wife (he had married Rosalia von Roeder, daughter of Lieutenant Ludwig A. S. von Roeder), Lieutenant L. A. S. von Roeder,[23] Louis Kleberg, Mrs. Otto von Roeder. Three sons of von Roeder and a daughter, together with a servant had preceded the party to Texas. The other passengers were mainly from the Duchy of Oldenburg. It took then sixty days to land in New Orleans. They finally landed at Galveston, December 22, 1834. During the War of Independence, Kleberg and his compatriots took part in the bloody storming of San Antonio. They later settled near Cat Spring, in Austin County. Kleberg held many offices in the State, and became a Confederate at the outbreak of the Civil War, but was unable to serve on account of his advanced age. Kleberg was a man of especial culture. Besides a knowledge of the classics, he was a master of three modern languages and read their literature in the original. He kept up his interest in literature to the very end. No country could help but be aided by the addition of settlers of such a character.[24]

There is an interesting letter by one of these early settlers. He gives a good picture of the voyage and of the settlement. On account of its early date, and from the fact that it has, to my knowledge, never been quoted, it is given in full; it is dated, "Settlement on Mill Creek, in Austin's Colony, State of Texas, New Mexico, February 1, 1832."

"In February of the previous year we embarked on a brig to

---

[22] *Texas Historical Quarterly*, Vol. II, p. 228, foot note. This is taken from notes written by Kleberg in 1876.

[23] He is styled Baron von Roeder in a letter from M. E. Kleberg, of Galveston, dated Nov. 5, 1904.

[24] For an account of the life of these settlers see *Texas Historical Quarterly*, Vols. I and II.

New Orleans. It was still winter on our departure from New York, then mild spring breezes blew upon us four days after our departure. Between Cuba and Florida, we had later real summer, and the whole sea voyage of a thousand miles over that part of the ocean, through the Bahama Islands, into the Gulf of Mexico, up to the mouth of the Mississippi, we lay constantly against the wind and came somewhat back. On the Mississippi up to New Orleans, a hundred and twenty miles (five make a German mile) we received favorable news of Austin's colony in Texas; we embarked again in the schooner of thirty-seven tons and landed after an eight-day voyage at Harris- burgh in this colony. Each immigrant who wishes to engage in farming receives a league of land; a single person, a one-quarter of a league.[25] A league is a league long and the same distance in width. He has in fees for surveying, cost of introduction, etc., to pay $160 in installments; he must take the oath of citizenship and is after a period of a year a citizen of the free United States of Mexico; also as Europeans, who are especially welcome, we received a peculiarly good league of land, and built upon it.

"The State of Texas in which our colony makes nearly the sixth part, lies in the south on the Gulf of Mexico between the 27 degree and 31 degree north latitude, in which also Napoleon's followers have settled. The rivers Trinidad, Rio Brassos (Brazos) and Rio Colorado flow through Austin's colony. It contains the chief city, San Felippe de Austin and the settlements of Harrisburgh, Bassoria (Brazoria), and Matagardo (Matagorda). One sails in three or four days to Tampico and Vera Cruz. The ground is hilly and alternates with forest and natural grass plains. Various kinds of trees. Climate like that of Sicily. The soil needs no fertilizer. Almost constant east wind. No winter, almost like March in Germany. Bees, birds and butterflies the whole winter through. A cow with a calf costs ten dollars. For ploughing, oxen are used. Planters who have seven hundred head of cattle are common. Principal products: Tobacco, rice, indigo (grows wild), sweet potatoes, melons of an especial goodness, watermelons, wheat, rye, vegetables of all kinds; peaches in great quantity grow wild in the woods; mulberries, many kinds of walnuts, wild plums, persimmons, sweet as honey; wine in great quantity, but not of a particular taste; honey is found chiefly in hollow trees. Birds of all kinds, from pelicans to humming birds. Wild prey such as: Deer, bears, raccoons, wild turkeys, geese, partridges (the latter as large as domestic fowls), etc., in quantity. Free hunting and fishing. Wild horses and buffalo in hordes; wolves, but of a feeble kind; also panthers and leopards, of which there is no danger; rich game, delicious roasts. Meadows with the most charming flowers. Many snakes, also rattlesnakes; each planter knows safe means against them. A league of land contains four thousand four hundred and forty acres of land, moun-

---

[25] This is evidently a mistake and should be one-half a league.

tain and valley, woods and meadows, cut through by brooks. Through many settlers at one point, the value of it rises so high in price, that it has already come to be sold at a dollar per acre. English the ruling speech. Slavery forbidden, but silently allowed. Day labor three-quarters to a dollar, with board. Clothing and shoes very dear. Each settler builds himself a block-house. The more children, the better for easy field labor. The same manner of life as in North America. Mosquitos and gnats only common on the coast. Formerly no, and later on only community taxes. Yearly scarcely three months work. No need for money, free exercise of religion, and the best markets for all products at the Mexican harbors; up the river there is much silver, but there are still Indian races there. We men satisfy ourselves with hunting and horse-races. On account of the better markets, many people have come here from Missouri. One should go from Bremen to New Orleans; from here to Harrisburgh, the cost is ten dollars per person; goods must be paid extra; children only cost half price; living utensils are bought in New Orleans; with favorable winds the journey lasts only four days. On account of the yellow fever, one should arrive in New Orleans some weeks before the month of July, or after the first of October. Arrived in Harrisburgh, wagons with oxen are rented to San Felippe where one reports to the land office; it is a good thing if one can speak English; only enough money is needed as is necessary to purchase a league of land. A father of a family must remember that he receives on his arrival, through the land granted to him, a county (Grafschaft), which will come to be worth in a short time, from seven to eight hundred (dollars), for which it is often sold here. The expenses for the land need not be paid immediately. Many raise the money from their cattle. For my acquaintances and former countrymen I have on my estate a stopping place until they have selected a league of land, which is not done so quickly. Col. Austin, however, promised recently to take care that German arrivals should be settled immediately. Who is unmarried, will bring a good sensible companion for life with him. He who is married knows that many children belong to wealth. Arrived at San Felippe, ask after Friedrich Ernst at Mill Creek. It is thirty miles from there and you will find me. In New Orleans are purchased good axes for cutting wood of merchant Martinstein, Rue de Chartres. He is a German, and he will take especial care that you have everything necessary, on the journey from San Felippe you must camp in the open air. You must not lack meal and meat, a pair of good boots and rifle, as well as a saddle are essential needs. The chief city of Texas is San Antonio on the Rio del Norte. Your friend, Fritz Dirks.

N. B. Passports are not necessary. Sons over seventeen have like part in the settlement of the land."[26]

---

[26] Achenbach, Hermann: *Tagebuch meiner Reise, in d. Nordamerikanischen Freistaaten oder das neue Kanaan.* Düsseldorf, 1835, pp. 132-135.

When the above was written I had not seen an article by Mr. L. F. La Frentz, of San Antonio, Texas, in *Deutsch-Texunische Monatshefte*, vol. 11, no. 4. This article contains a resumé of the letter which Fritz Ernst sent to his compatriots in Germany and which was published in a newspaper in the Duchy of Oldenburg. The similarity of the Ernst letter to that quoted above leads me to believe that either the author of the work in which the letter signed Fritz Dirks is quoted either misunderstood the name or that the name Dirks is a misprint and should read Ernst. In many paragraphs the words of the two letters are identical. The letter of Ernst as stated above had a great influence on German immigration.

Many Germans were participants in the Texan War of Independence. The idea of battling against political tyranny and for religious freedom appealed to their revolutionary feelings. Undoubtedly this war with its romantic history later drew many Germans to Texas. It was, doubtless, aided by the publication by a German in that language of the history of the war. This history was a narrative of the personal experiences of the author in many of its engagements. It appeared[27] under different titles, and evidently had a large circulation in Germany as many copies are still extant. The author was born at Marienwerder. He was the son of the royal Prussian counsellor to the government, Wilhelm von Ehrenberg. As a member of "the Burchenschaft," at Jena, he was forced to come to America. At the outbreak of the Texan war he was in New Orleans and enlisted in the first company of the "New Orleans Grays," of which company many Germans were members. He was active in the storming of San Antonio and "the Alamo." After various adventures, he came with "the Grays" under the command of the unfortunate Colonel Fannin, and took part in the Goliad disaster and was one of the few to escape from that bloody encounter. He describes his experiences in a very dramatic manner, and his work must have had a strong influence over his German compatriots in the

---

[27] Ehrenberg, Hermann: *Texas und die Revolution, von Hermann Ehrenberg, Bürger der Republik;* Leipzig, 1843; *Der Freiheitskampf in Texas,* 1844; *Fahrten und Schicksale eines Deutschen in Texas,* 1845.

Fatherland; how much this one story led the romantic German, who was seeking adventure and was without doubt charmed by the life described in Ehrenberg's works to thoughts of immigration, it would be difficult to say. Bracht, in his work[28] mentions Ehrenberg as one of the authors to be read about Texas. Later Ehrenberg became a topographical surveyor in the surveying corps of the United States. He published his reports and letters about southern Arizona (1855-1860).[29] Among others who were participants in the Texan Revolution, were Dr. Gustav Busen,[30] Peter Mattern, George Curtmann, George Voss, Ed. Harkort, who was chief engineer on the staff of Houston, and held the rank of colonel; Franz Dieterich, who was one of the survivors of the Fannin disaster, March, 1836; George B. Erath, after whom "Erath County" is named, and who was a member of the legislature; Joseph Biegel, who founded Biegel's settlement;[31] Dr. Wilhelm Langenheim and Ferdinand Lindheimer. Of these, Voss and Curtmann, who had been Jena students, lost their lives at Goliad, March 27, 1836.[32] The two latter deserve separate mention. The former, Wilhelm Langenheim, came to America in 1830, and had been some years previous a lawyer in his native city of Braunschweig. He came to New York and joined a colony of Irish and Germans who intended to form a settlement on Aransas Bay, Texas. When the Texan War with Mexico broke out, he enlisted and showed skill in the storming of San Antonio. He shot the only cannon which the Texans possessed. He fell into the hands of the Mexicans during the expedition of Colonel Grant at San Patricio. Langenheim was one of the two who escaped to Matamoras. He was there taken prisoner and languished ten months in a Mexican prison. He was saved from being killed by the influence of a Spanish woman. In 1837, he took part in the war against the Seminoles, fighting a year and a half in all engagements. Later he settled in Philadel-

---

[28] Bracht, Viktor: *Texas im Jahre*, 1848, p. 308.
[29] Cf. Koerner, pp. 362-363.
[30] For a sketch of his life cf. *ibid*, p. 252. His life was most dramatic. A good illustration of the German revolutionist of the thirties.
[31] For a list of these Germans cf. Rosenberg, Kritik, p. 7.
[32] For a list of Germans in Texan Revolution cf. Appendix A.

phia, and in 1846[33] returned to Texas. He later returned to Philadelphia.

Ferdinand Jakob Lindheimer is one of the most notable figures among the early Germans in Texas. He was born in Frankfurt am Main in 1801,[34] and was seventy-eight years old at his death. He had studied at Jena, and perfected himself in pedagogy at Berlin. He was a teacher in many schools in Germany and was a personal friend of Goethe's Zuleika, Marianne Willemer, with whom he corresponded. He came to America in 1834 and was a member of the Latin settlement in St. Clair County, Illinois, and later joined the colony of Sartorius in Mexico. In 1835 he went to Texas to take part in its War of Independence. He took part in all its engagements up to the battle of San Jacinto. After the war he settled in Texas and was used by Prince Solms-Braunfels and later by von Meusebach in the "Adelscolonie," at New Braunfels. He lived in this city until his death. He was the editor of the *New Braunfels Zeitung* from 1853 until 1869. During his life in Texas, he became known in Europe as a botanist. He collected a great number of specimens and sent them to Germany. He was one of the best known naturalists of his day. Many botanical specimens were named after him "Lindheimeriana."[35] He was aided in his work by a queer character of the name of Friedrich.[36] The latter was peculiar in his dress and lived as a hermit. He and Lindheimer went to Mexico after the Texan War. Friedrich was a student of law in Germany and came to Texas in 1834. For forty years he studied in Texas with the greatest assiduity. The University of Leipzig offered a prize for the best monograph on, and newest discoveries in, entomology. Friedrich sent a complete work in Latin with a rich collection of beetles, butterflies and

---

[33] Roemer met Langenheim during his stay in Texas. The account given by Roemer is probably from an account furnished him by Langenheim. Cf. Roemer, p. 205; also Koerner, p. 361. Koerner's account is either based upon Roemer, or a similar account given by Langenheim.

[34] Koerner says he was born in 1802. Dr. Siemering, who was a personal friend, says the date was 1801. Cf. Koerner, p. 362; *Deutsche Pionier*, Vol. II, No. 10, p. 381, article by Dr. A. Siemering.

[35] Cf. Roemer, p. 425ff; *Texas Historical Quarterly*, II, pp. 172-173; *Deutsche Pionier*, Vol. II, No. 10, p. 381; Koerner, p. 364.

[36] Cf. *Deutsche Pionier* as supra; also, Vol. 12, No. 10, pp. 394-5.

insects of all kinds and received the prize. Later, he and Lindheimer returned to Texas and devoted themselves to their chosen studies.

Among the settlements between the Brazos and Colorado, founded from 1833-1836 are those of Shelby, founded by the von Roeder family; Frelsburg, family of Frels, Oldenburger; Industry, founded by Ernst and Fordtran.[37]

That there were many Germans settled in the State before the great stream of immigration in the forties is shown by the mention of German arrivals in the newspapers of the State. The *Houston Telegraph,* December 11, 1839, mentions the arrival of forty families of German immigrants, and states that four hundred families of that nation may be expected before January first of the following year. The same paper, under date of September 14, 1842, announces the arrival of Counts Joseph de Boos-Waldeck and Victor de Leiningen. They had come to arrange for the later immigration made by the "Adelsverein." The *Civilian and Galveston Gazette,* January 7, 1843, announces the arrival from Havre on the ship "Ebro" of one hundred and seventeen immigrants. The *Telegraph*[38] reports that some sixty families had arrived at Galveston; that they were all farmers and intended to settle in the interior. The influence of Ernst is seen in that many of these immigrants are bound for the interior and intended to settle on Mill Creek. The same paper under date of December 27, 1843, and January 17, 1844, notes the arrival of fifty-two and a hundred and twenty-nine immigrants, respectively. Like those noted above, they were intending settling on Mill Creek.

What the condition of these early German immigrants rose to be is shown by statements of the arrivals in the thirties and their success within five or ten years. Several had come without any means of support and were worth from $3,000 to $5,000 in cash, besides owning a league of land, have hogs, cattle and horses and good houses. Their skill, industry and energy are especially marked.[39] These illustrations are sufficient to show

---
[37] Mgebroff, p. 2.
[38] Houston *Telegraph,* Feb. 1, 1843.
[39] *Civilian and Galveston Gazette,* Dec. 2, 1843.

the character of the early German inhabitant in this State. That he must have exerted a strong influence in developing the Texan Republic is shown by his loyalty and patriotism during its War of Independence. That many were men of culture and refinement is indicated clearly by the examples of such men as Kleberg, the von Roeders, Langenheim, Ehrenberg and Lindheimer. That their love of music was not given up with their leaving the Fatherland is shown by the fact that some had pianos.[40]

West of the Colorado River there were no noteworthy German settlements before 1844.[41]

---

[40] Texas Quarterly, Vol. I, p. 298
[41] Rosenberg, *Kritik*, p. 7.

CHAPTER III.

THE SOCIETY OF GERMAN PRINCES AND NOBLES FORMED FOR THE PURPOSE OF AIDING GERMANS TO SETTLE IN TEXAS. ITS AIMS. ITS INFLUENCE ON GERMAN IMMIGRATION.

It has been previously shown that before the forties many Germans had already settled in Texas. With the early forties immigration to Texas began in great numbers. One year the number landing in Galveston is stated as 8,000;[1] and in three months alone 4,020 Germans landed at that port. The motives which enticed such a number of immigrants to choose Texas for their home; the influences which brought about emigration en masse; the character of the emigrants themselves—their rank and position; the many sad instances resulting from such an immense immigration: these make the story one of as absorbing interest as the undertaking in itself was novel. Of all the colonial experiments attempted in this country, probably none had such a peculiar history as the one about to be told. The story in brief accounts has been told by many a German traveller and by as many more who never even saw the shores of America.[2] The accounts in English have been meagre, and of only brief mention. Those deserving special notice are Olmsted, "Texas Journeys"; an article in Tait's *Edinburgh Magazine* for 1848, and an article by Ferdinand Kapp in the New York *Tribune*, January 20, 1855. The story is also interesting because it shows what an important part literature played in inducing the Germans to emigrate. As the colonists in the early Colonial period were induced by the descriptions of life in America, as one dramatist of the time said, that "all the streets were of massy gold," so the colored pictures of life in Texas, the freedom of the inhabitant, led thousands to settle in Texas. The influence of Duden's work has been told in a previous chapter. It is also interesting to note that among the

---
[1] Cf. *supra*, Ch. I, p. 2.
[2] Soergel in his work, *Neueste Nachrichten aus Texas, Eisleben*, 1847, says that the author of the work entitled, *Texas Rathgeber für Auswanderer von Kuno Damian Schutz, Vereinsbeamten in Neu braunfels*, Weisbaden, 1846, had never set foot in Texas. Others could be mentioned.

first German settlers, the one who probably was the first to bring his family to Texas was incited to emigrate to America after having read that book. His pictures in turn brought other immigrants. The Texan revolution, with its many thrilling stories, the struggle of a handful of hardy settlers against tyranny and religious oppression; the dramatic accounts of "the Alamo", of "Goliad" and "San Jacinto" became known throughout the reading public, not only of this country, but of Europe also. Many of those partaking in its engagements were Germans. These may have sent letters home, and in this way had an influence on immigration. Be this as it may, one writer's influence was particularly strong. This was the anonymous writer Sealsfield. His real name was Carl Postl. He was born March 3, 1793, in the village of Poppitz, Austria, and died in Switzerland in 1864. His father was mayor and justice of the town. He himself became secretary of the Kreuzherren von Poeltenberg in 1816. On account of trouble, he fled in 1823 to the United States. He travelled extensively in this country, and is supposed to have been a plantation owner in Louisiana. He became a most prolific writer. His descriptive powers were uncommon; his knowledge of life and character of every kind exceptional. "His historical novels are based on original research; his tales of the present time give us the fruit of his own observation and personal experience, beyond which the author had no desire to go."[3] It is stated that "in the fortress of the Bund at Mainz some officers and nobles whiled away the time by reading. Among the works was that of the latest romance, 'The Cabin Book' of the beloved writer, Sealsfield, which caused a furore in all circles of Germany.[4]" Bracht mentions his work among those worthy of mention regarding Texas.[5] Kapp says that the Society of Nobles was influenced by the fact that Prince zu Leiningen had read during a sickness many works praising Texas.[6] That Seals-

---

[3] Faust, *Sealsfield*, p. 43.

[4] Rosenberg, *Kritik*, Austin, 1894, p. 13. Rosenberg was an early settler of Texas. His uncle was the Rosenberg mentioned above.

[5] Bracht, *Texas im Jahre* 1848, 1849, p. 308; also cf. Gottschall, Rudolf, *Die deutsche National Literatur des neunzehnten Jahrhunderts*. Article on "Sealsfield and the Ethnographische Roman or Exotische Culturroman."

[6] Kapp, *Aus und über Amerika*, Pt. II, p. 247.

field's novels were among these is very probable. In 1837 appeared his work, "Nathan the Squatter; or, the First American in Texas."⁷ His descriptions of pioneer life are picturesque in the extreme, and some of them are almost idyllic. It is not to be marvelled at that they aroused a spirit of adventure in "the young Germans" of that time, who, to use the expression then current, were Europamüde. He gives idyllic scenes of life in the then thinly populated territory of Texas. Here is a description of scenery that must have been novel to his German readers:

"The colony * * * extended from southeast to northwest along the summit of a ridge about fifteen miles in length, rising about seventy feet from the river on the southern side, and gradually sloping away to the prairie on the north. On the level summit of the ridge were situated the plantations of the wealthier members of society; and a more beautiful, or more favorable settlement you could not imagine. On one side lay what are called clearing lands, from which the primitive forest had just been removed—on the other, immense prairies with the tall grass waving about the heads of the browsing cattle, and horses who were pulling and tumbling against each other like rolling stones; the sound of tinkling cow-bells came to our ears on the gentle breeze; and in the far blue distance, a thick fog was seen glimmering in the sunbeams through every opening of the vast forest. The whole scene was buried in the profoundest silence—save only the tinkling cowbells, and occasionally the heavy blast of the sea-shell calling the workmen home from the fields. There was something charming and irresistible in the landscape. We paused * * * after having contemplated the magnificent scene for several minutes in silence. * * *

"Here these once magnificent trees—the best adapted for ship timbers of any in the world—were burned solely for their ashes. In France, a single one of these trunks would have sold for a thousand livres.⁸ * * *

"With the wreck of our fortune, as little as it was competent to support us at home, here it was amply sufficient to gratify every wish of the heart—here I could prepare a home for my betrothed far from the injuries and storms of the world. If the French, the Spanish and the Germans, with far less means, had succeeded in this country, and placed themselves on an equality with the wealthiest in the land, surely I could do the same. I was as yet young, active and enterprising, actuated by faith and love, and feeling a

---
⁷ *Nathan, der Squatter Regulator, oder der erste Amerikaner in Texas.* Zurich, 1837; translated into English. *Life in the New World.* Translated by Hebbe and Mackay. New York, J. Winchester, 1844, Part 5.
⁸ Translation, p. 326ff.

world of power within me. Nothing was wanting but a little instruction—a tutor, to set me to work. * * * I knew nothing about agriculture, except so far as it had been necessary to tenants and stewards, or rather to receive the rents they handed over to us. I could purchase a plantation and manage it by means of agents; but even if I had capital enough for this I knew none of the planters, and must be dependent on my own household; and to venture all on the cast of this die, which in the first year might ruin me, would have been downright insanity. * * *

"Here on this second plantation, I found the thing I had so long searched in vain elsewhere—the guide capable of conducting me to the desired goal. * * * I found the rudiments—the A B C of squatter life—in the clearings, in the woodland, and in the live oaks; the spelling book in the rude and artless dwellings, in the rough furniture made by the backwoodsman himself, in the horses and in the corn-stubbles. I saw plainly that I had only to do as the squatters had done to accomplish the same ends. He only who has to solve the difficult problem of getting along in the backwoods, as they term it, can form an idea of the childish haste I pounced on every object. To me it was an embryo plantation. The log-house had irresistible charms. I was in an ecstasy at the thought of the time when my beloved family, in their plain and simple robes, should come to meet me at the cabin-door as I returned from the fields."

Such descriptions as these must have set the minds of the ambitious young Germans to thoughts of immigration. In 1841 appeared the work which, if we can accept our sources, had the great influence of resulting in emigration to Texas en masse. This was, "Das Kajütenbuch, oder Schilderungen aus dem Leben in Texas," Zürich, 1841.[9] The lively descriptions of the Texan War of Independence, the pictures of plantation life and of the extraordinary fruitfulness of the soil—all could not help but leave an impression on the sentimental German people.[10] It contains such pictures of the life and scenery in Texas as the following:

"Mr. Neal had only been three years in the country, and had during that time devoted himself exclusively to cattle, an occupation which, in Texas, is one of the pleasantest, most profitable and easiest which any gentleman can undertake without derogating from his dignity. His herds consisted of about seven or eight hundred head of cattle, and from fifty to sixty horses, all mustangs. The

---

[9] It had many translations. The most common is that by Mersch, N. Y., 1844. For others see Faust, *Sealsfield*, p. 53.

[10] Cf. Ch. XVI of the book for his account of the Texan War of Independence including the Alamo massacre, the Goliad distaster, and the battle of San Jacinto.

plantation, like most of those we had seen, was as yet little improved; the log-house built in that style which is so common in our Southwestern States, was spacious and comfortable. It was standing on the skirt of an island, * * * between two gigantic sycamore trees, which sheltered it from the sun and wind. Before it, the endless prairie, with its waving grass and flowers, extended to an immeasureable distance; in the background rose a Texian primitive forest in its glorious majesty, overgrown with grape vines climbing a hundred feet or more among the trees and spreading their shoots all over the island. These islands are one of the most attractive beauties of Texian land scenery, and so exceedingly different in their shapes, and the luxury of their trees, that after having been for years in the country you will find new beauties in them.

"They are circular, in the shape of a parallelogram, of a hexagon, or an octagon, or else coiled up like snakes; the most skillful landscape gardener would vainly attempt to imitate these manifold charming figures. In the morning or towards the evening, when surrounded by light frames of vapors resembling blue silk, and shining in the trembling light of the first or last rays of the sun, they present a picture which would enrapture the least poetical soul.

"The easy, unassuming hospitality of the inhabitants of this favored country is another feature not less worthy of an idyl. Even in those houses where we came without recommendations—and I do not mean to speak of letters, but of verbal recommendations or compliments—we entered without ceremony quite unceremoniously, just as if we had been old acquaintances."[11] * * * "As to the Texians, I firmly believe that if the whole Mexican army had marched against them, they would just as quietly and cheerfully have cleaned their rifles. The only words that were spoken were: spare your powder and lead—do not lose a shot."[12]

These quotations will suffice for Sealsfield. What their effect would have been upon the young German noblemen in Mainz will be left to the reader to imagine. Other works which were current in Germany at this time were those of Kennedy and of Scherpf.[13] Kennedy was for several years previous to 1846 English Consul in Galveston. Roemer[14] met Kennedy himself

---

[11] Translation, *ibid*, pp. 10-11.
[12] *Ibid*, p. 77.
[13] Kennedy: *Texas, its History, Geography, Natural History, and Topography.* 2 Vols. London, 1840. It was translated into German by Otto von Czarnowsky, Frankfurt a. M., 1846. Scherpf, G. A.: *Entstehungsgeschichte und gegenwärtiger Zustand des neuen unabhängigen amerikanischen Staats Texas. Ein Beitrag zur Geschichte, Statistik und Geographie dieses Jahrhunderts, im Lande selbst gesammelt von G. A. Scherpf.* Augsburg, 1841.
[14] Roemer. p. 60. For character of the work cf. Roemer. p. 43.

in Texas. He says that Kennedy's work had spread almost the first knowledge of this land hitherto unknown in Europe.

Scherpf's work is mentioned by Roemer,[15] also by other German writers about Texas.[16] Scherpf [17] says that Texas is larger than all the German States, including Bohemia and Switzerland; that it has a climate similar to that of Italy; that in fruitfulness and beauty of formation none of the European countries could compare with it; that if it were presented to a few thousand persons, a state could be formed; that hunting and fishing are free in Texas, and can be found at any time of the year wild near the cities. His book contains chapters on the history of the Texan Revolution, products, rivers, business, etc. He says that the climate is almost continual summer; "altho the land flows with milk and honey, the cows must be milked and the honey gathered." It seems probable that Hecke's book must have been read by some of the German nobles, as the program of the German "Adelsverein" contains almost similar statements to those contained in that work. The Society published an account of its program. It stated that after having studied numerous geographical and statistical books about Texas, they "have come to the conclusion that in relation to climate, fertility of the soil and easiness of possession, it offers to the emigrant more advantages than any other land on earth." [18]

THE GERMAN ADELSVEREIN.

The late thirties and the early forties were a period of transition. It was the period when all sorts of idealistic experiments were being tried. Saint Simon and Fourier had many disciples both in Europe and America. During the forties, Fourierism had its sway in the United States. Horace Greeley was one of the advocates of "Association.' The *Tribune* gave up its columns to expositions on the benefits of community life. Charles A. Dana, George William Curtis, Emerson and other leaders of

---

[15] Roemer, p. 43.
[16] Notably Kordül, 1846, in his sources.
[17] Preface of Scherpf.
[18] *Handbuch für deutsche Auswanderer.* Bremen, 1846, p. 114.

the day were advocates of the benefits of that kind of life. The "Brook Farm" experiment and the Icarian communities were examples of the tendencies of the times.[19] It was during this time that there was formed a society of German nobles for the settlement of Texas by Germans. The immigration was to be in large numbers and the immigrants were to settle at one point, thus preserving their identity. The organization was to form a society *inter pares;* that is, only those of noble rank were to be members of it. On April 20, 1842, there gathered at Biebrich a. Rhein princes and counts and subscribed to the following document:[20]

"We the undersigned explain through this, that we having as our aim the purchase of land in the free-state of Texas, have constituted ourselves under this date, as a society. Biebrich, April 20, 1842."

The Count of Castell was the leading spirit of the undertaking. Among the members were Graf Castell, Graf Boos-Waldeck and many other noblemen. On the same date it was decided to send Counts Boos-Waldeck and Victor zu Leiningen to Texas to visit the country and purchase land. In May, 1842, they journeyed to Texas with money and full powers to carry out the ideas of the Society. They arrived in Galveston some time previous to September, 1842.[21] At this time the president of the Republic of Texas was, through law of February 5, 1842, empowered to grant land to colonists under certain conditions.[22] Leiningen [23] laid down conditions (exemption from taxes for many years) which the president could not accept. Leiningen returned to Germany in 1843 and reported in favor of colonization in great numbers, in spite of his failure in Texas. On February 4, 1841, a contract was entered into between W. G. Peters and others with the government of Texas, by which colonists could

---

[19] Cf. Hilquit, *Socialism in the United States.*
[20] Rosenberg, *Kritik,* p. 9. *Entwickelungs-Geschichte,* etc., p. 23
[21] The *Houston Post,* Sept. 14, 1842, notes that they had arrived in town Sept. 10, 1842.
[22] Hartley's *Digest,* Art. 2087.
[23] Cf. Rosenberg, *Kritik,* p. 10; *Entwickelungs-Geschichte,* p. 24. See above.

be settled in Texas. This act gave the president of Texas the authority to grant lands to W. G. Peters and others introducing emigrants into Texas. On February 5, 1842, these rights were extended to others. The president was empowered to introduce colonists under certain terms as he thought suitable.[24] Had Leiningen entered into such an agreement, it is very probable that the future disasters of the German "Adelsverein" would not have resulted.

Boos-Waldeck [25] bought an extraordinarily favorable piece of land in Fayette County for 56,000 gulden. It contained good wood and water and showed the practical side of the purchaser. The land consisted of a league and was situated on Jack Creek, about fifteen miles from the Colorado River. He made of this a cotton plantation and worked it with about thirty slaves.[26] He was recalled, and returned in January, 1844, and reported against emigration en masse, because there was not enough money for that kind of an undertaking.

In the meantime, during June, 1843, a stock company, with forty shares of 5,000 gulden ($2,000) par value per share, was formed. The entire capital stock was 200,000 gulden ($80,000).[27] The purpose of the company was the purchase and settlement of land areas in Texas. Castell was strongly in favor of emigration en masse. He was influenced by the idea of the English East India Company.[28] Boos-Waldeck's advice was not accepted and he left the Society. Accordingly, on March 25, 1844, in a general assembly, there was formed the "Gesellschaft zum Schutze deutscher Auswanderer nach Texas." This became generally called the "Mainzer Adelsverein," or more simply the "Adelsverein." [29] The Verein consisted of the following twenty-one members: Herzog Adolph von Nassau, Her-

---

[24] Cf. Hartley's *Digest*, Art. 2087. Dallam's *Reports*, No. XXX, pp. 326,327.
[25] Cf. Rosenberg, p. 10. *Entwickelungs-Geschichte*, p. 24. Kapp, *Aus und über Amerika*, Pt. II, p. 250.
[26] Kapp, p. 250.
[27] Cf. Rosenberg, p. 10. *Entwickelungs-Geschichte*, p. 25. *Answers to Interrogatories*, pp. 4 and 5 (an account by Meusebach, later director general in Texas), Austin, 1894.
[28] Rosenberg, p. 10.
[29] *Entwickelungs-Geschichte*, p. 25. Kapp, p. 251-252.

zog Bernhard Erich von Meiningen, Herzog August Ernst von Sachsen-Coburg, Prinz Friedrich Wilhelm Ludwig von Preussen, Fürst Günther zu Schwarzburg-Rudolstadt, Fürst Karl von Leiningen, Fürst Hermann von Wied, Fürst Ferdinand von Solms-Braunfels, Prinz Franz von Colorado-Mansfeld, Prinz Otto Viktor von Schönberg-Waldenburg, Prinz zu Solms-Braunfels Rheingrafenstein, Prinz Alexander von Solms-Braunfels, Graf Christian von Neu-Leiningen-Westerburg, Graf Friedrich von Alt-Leiningen-Westerburg, Graf Viktor von Alt-Leiningen-Westerburg, Graf Karl von Issenburg-Meerholz, Graf Edmund von Hatzfeld, Graf Karl Wilhelm George von Inn und Knyphausen-Lutelsberg, Graf Ormand von Rennesse, Graf Karl von Castell and Baron Paul Szirnay.[30] Count von Castell was the recognized head of the undertaking. He declared that on the 25th. of March, 1844, in the general assembly, it was decided to give up the idea of private purchase of land and as an aim it was decided, financial speculation excepted, to furnish aid and protection to the Germans emigrating to Texas.[31] The Society was incorporated May 3, 1845, under a ministerial rescript of the Duchy of Nassau. The aims of the Society were set forth in a pamphlet issued in 1845.[32] The program as set forth in that pamphlet is as follows:

"An association has been formed having for its aim as much as possible to guide German emigration into one and that a favorable channel, to support the emigrant on his long journey, and in his first struggles to assist him in getting a home.

"The association publishes this advertisement not with any view to procure money towards their undertaking, the necessary capital having been already signed, but, conscious of a righteous purpose, they feel it due to themselves and the public, to lay before the latter the motives which have called their association into existence; the ways and means by which they hope to effect their object, and the principles by which they are guided.

"The association neither means to further, nor excuse the

---

[30] The German titles are given to show the distinction between Prinz and Fürst.

[31] *Die deutschen Ansiedelungen in Texas*, Bonn, 1845, p. 4.

[32] This pamphlet is contained in the book published by the Verein, *Ein Handbuch für deutsche Auswanderer*, Bremen, 1846. An earlier edition was published, Bremen, 1845. Cf. Edition of 1846, pp. 64 and ff. The translation is taken from the article in Tait's Edinburgh Magazine.

tendency to emigrate. Enough that it exists, which is, unfortunately, as little to be denied as it is to be checked. Many causes work to bring this about. The work of hand-labor being suppressed by machinery; the great, almost periodic, crises that overwhelm commerce; the increasing poverty consequent upon over-population, the diminution of labor, and, also perhaps the much lauded richness of the soil in the New World; but, above all, an expectation, sometimes realized, but fully as often deceived, of a happier lot across the sea. Under such circumstances, the emigrants certainly could not fail to better themselves if keeping together in a well-ordered mass, and placing themselves under proper guidance, they found protection and support abroad. Thus are the necessity for, and aims of the association, at once explained. It wishes to regulate and guide emigration that a chance may be afforded the Germans of finding in America a German home, and that by maintaining an unbroken connection between themselves and the old country, an industrial and commercial intercourse may arise, morally and materially beneficial to both. It is after this manner that the association wishes to contribute its mite towards Germany's glory, and prosperity, and perhaps at some future period to afford the German poor a field for rewarded labor, to open to German industry new markets and to give to German sea-trade a 'wider expansion'." [33]

This document was published after annexation to the United States seemed probable. Other writers have given other motives as the purpose of the Verein. Von Behr in 1847 said that the Verein wished to form a feudal state which would lend money to its settlers and they would be treated, in a way, as its own property.[34] Mrs. Ernst, who entertained Leiningen, Boos-Waldeck and Solms-Braunfels, says that they had the idea of forming Texas into a German colony and of organizing a monarchy there. Her husband informed them that this would be a difficult task since Texas was too near the American republic.[35] Grund says that they desired to Germanize the colony and to make a German state in America.[36] Berghaus says that it is the talk that the nobles planned to keep their subjects in the same condition of custom and habit as they had in Germany; that they would emigrate to America with all their subjects (Un-

[33] This program will be found in the original in Appendix B. It will also be found in Kapp, p. 252ff, and in Kordül, p. 254ff.
[34] Von Behr, Ottomar, 1847, p. 105. Behr lived in Texas many years. Cf. Olmsted, *Texas Journeys*, p. 193 foot-note.
[35] *Der deutsche Pionier*, Vol. XVI, No. 9, from *Texan Post*.
[36] Grund, F. J., *Handbuch*, Stuttgart, 1846, p. 262.

terthanen oder Hintersassen).³⁷ He also states that the Mainzer Verein should be numbered among the colonies founded on philanthropic motives. A recent writer on the Evangelical Church in Texas says that the choice fell on the newly founded State of Texas where it was hoped to strengthen the already strong influence of the Germans on the government, and if possible in course of time to succeed in getting the Germans to control the state entirely.³⁸ It is stated that England was back of the movement to form a colony in Texas.³⁹ It is even said to have gone so far that a contract was drawn up between the English Government and the Verein. By it the Verein agreed to place 10,000 families in Texas, the English Government to guarantee protection to the colony. A new market for British goods, a new source of cotton opposition to slavery and the extension of the area to the United States were the reason for this. Prince Leiningen was the half brother of Queen Victoria. Prince Solms-Braunfels was a student friend, at Bonn, of Prince Albert. Kapp says that during his stay in Texas he often heard it stated that Lord Palmerston through Prince Albert had chosen Texas as the best colonization field to establish, under the protection of the English Government and in aristocratic feudal interests, a European and especially a Germany colony. This was in course of time to become a dam against the growing power of the United States. He further states that after search he has not been able to find any proof for the assertion and is convinced of the unreasonableness of the statement.⁴⁰ He asserts that reliable information is not yet known and in the foreground stands the philanthropic motive.⁴¹ The original reports of the Prince Solms-Braunfels, the commissioner-general of the Verein in Texas, to the parent society in Germany show that the motives that influenced the German noblemen to colonization were in part commercial and in part humanistic. These reports were written

---

³⁷ Berghaus, Heinrich, Dr., *Die Vereinigten Staaten von Nord Amerika*, Gotha, 1848, p. 78ff.
³⁸ Mgebroff, pp. 3 and 4.
³⁹ Cf. Olmsted, *Texas Journeys*, p. 172, foot-note.
⁴⁰ Kapp, p. 249.
⁴¹ *Ibid*, p. 248.

by the Prince for the eyes of the directory in German alone, and they show the Utopian character of the whole colonization movement. They show that "the Verein" was greatly influenced by the idea of maintaining their own nationality among the German settlers in Texas. They aimed to concentrate the Germans in one locality and that near enough to the coast to control the trade with Mexico. In one report, Prince Solms reports a conversation with Bourgeois d'Orvanne. The latter said: *"Pah! Nationalité c'est un mot."* To which Solms replied: *"Oui, pour vous peut-être, pas pour moi, ni pour l'association."* In another report, Solms claims that the Germans in Texas recognized as the aims of the Adelsverein, the preservation of German nationality in that republic. While Solms was at Industry, Fritz Ernst gave as a toast: "To the welfare of the noble and generous German princes who also consider the welfare of their subjects on this side of the ocean." The Prince reports that it is his greatest desire to obtain from the Texan Congress such commercial privileges for "the Verein" as would place it in condition not only to care for the agricultural classes in the Fatherland, but also would gain for German industry new markets and for German commerce a wider expansion. He promises to obtain from the Texan Congress "a reduction of all import duties for all ships sailing under the protection of 'the Verein'." He states that the people of the West recognize that through the relations of the Adelsverein with Texas cheaper merchandise may be obtained. The Prince wished to visit Germany in the spring of 1845, in order to disclose "the opportunities for colonization as well as for business which can be carried under the flag of "the Verein," and to make known to the German government the commercial advantages which would accrue to them as a result of their subjects becoming members of the society.[42] The majority of the statements attributing the motives of the founders of the Society to the influence of British gold can be traced to a certain A. Siemering.[43] He was a fanatic hater of princes

---

[42] The reports of Prince Solms-Braunfels are printed in *Deutsch-texanische Monatshefte*, Vol. 9. They were discovered by its editor in an inn in New Braunfels.

[43] Letter of L. F. La Freutz, editor of *Deutsch-texanische Monatshefte*,

and all nobility. His accounts were full of bias and prejudice.[44] *Turn Zeitung*, of 1853, states that Solms-Braunfels had the patronage of Queen Victoria to aid him in his Adelsverein; that the princes were to form a young dynasty under the protection of the German Bund.[45] A careful sifting of the proof will probably show that in the main the reasons for the founding of the Verein were philanthropic, although it probably had some ideas of commercial benefits to be derived, and the idea of founding a German state in Texas may not have been absent. The proof for the latter motive can be traced to earlier statements than the statement that British gold was back of the movement. No earlier statement has yet been found than that of 1853. Siemering did not come to Texas until the early fifties. There is no doubt that eagerness for land played an important part in inducing emigrants to settle in Texas.[46] The idea that there were minerals in that territory also had its influence.[47]

In the same pamphlet, specified above, it is further stated that after careful study of different works about Texas, that territory was fixed upon as the most suitable to their purpose. They announce that they have a district of land 450 square miles [48] in extent not very far from San Antonio. Of this land each emigrant was to receive a stated portion [49]—320 acres for each family or 160 for each single man over seventeen years of age, as a free gift, upon arrival, without being expected either then or at some future time to refund for it to the association. This gift was to be secured by documents before departure, to become the property of the emigrant as soon as he should have dwelt three consecutive years on the allotment, the returns of the land belonging to him from the very first. The Verein further promised to provide good and roomy ships for the passage;

---

[44] Same letter, *supra*.
[45] *Turn Zeitung, Organ des socialistischen Turnerbundes*, N. Y., Sept. 5, 1853, p. 277.
[46] Sommer, 1846, p. 2.
[47] Ross, 1851, p. 44.
[48] Cf. Appendix C.
[49] *Ibid*.

cheap, yet a wholesome, fare whilst on board ship; agents to receive the emigrants on landing; and carriages to transport them and their baggage free of expense, to their place of destination. Their wants on arrival were to be no less cared for—houses, or the means to erect such, were to be immediately provided, and all the necessary tools for husbandry, cattle for stocking farms, necessary provisions and eatables, until such time as they could raise such articles for themselves. All these first necessities of the newly arrived settler were to be procured at the storehouse belonging to the association, not only at lower prices than they could be gotten elsewhere, but upon credit. They were furthermore promised churches and schools, physicians and apothecaries, and a hospital. Added to all these advantages was that of the emigrant being able, if unsatisfied, to return to Europe in the ships of the Verein, and pay no more for the homeward than the outward voyage. To obviate the possible difficulties and loss attending upon money-changing on arriving, the Verein also offered to accept deposits in Europe, which it would refund in Texas. In another paragraph it was stated that each person should deposit 300 fl. ($120) in Bremen, each family 600 fl. ($240). For this sum the Verein promised free passage from Bremen to the port of landing, free transportation to the colony itself; and the delivery of a dwelling house. If the emigrant should deposit a larger sum, the Verein promised 3% interest on such deposit. It further promised that a savings bank would be established which would pay 5% interest. The right of choosing their own officials was left to the colonists in accordance with the laws of Texas.[50] Previous to the publication of the program, a certain Frenchman by the name of d'Orvanne[51] had come to Germany. This was in the summer of 1843. He had a colonization contract and on September 19, 1843, the Verein bought his rights from him. He was made a member of the Verein, and was chosen as colonial-director. Prince Charles, of Solms-Braunfels, was chosen as general agent on March 25, 1844, and d'Or-

---

[50] Cf. Appendix C. *Organische Statut der Colonisation.*
[51] Alexander Bourgeois (d'Orvanne).

vanne was to aid him in Texas in carrying out the scheme of the society.[52] The program given above had been adopted April 9, 1844. The contract of d'Orvanne had still three months to run. His contract was dated June 3, 1842, and under its conditions within eighteen months four hundred families had to settle in the territory of his grant. The contract was therefore abrogated December 3, 1843. Through law of January 30, 1844, all contracts whose terms had remained unfilled were abrogated. In the meantime, in May, 1844, d'Orvanne and Solms-Braunfels journeyed to Texas. The latter arrived at Galveston July 1, 1844.[53] Arrived in Texas, d'Orvanne prayed the president in a letter under date of July 8 and 10, 1844, to have his contracts extended. He could not conceal longer from Prince Solms-Braunfels the real truth regarding his contract. The prince addressed letters to the "Verein" showing the real condition of affairs.[54] The arrival of immigrants was approaching, and there was no land in sight.

In these letters, the prince states regarding the plantation of Nassau which had been already purchased by Boos-Waldeck that it was not suited to the purposes of the colonization society; he also states regarding Bourgeois d'Orvanne's grant that it was too far from the coast in order to carry on trade with Mexico; that it was in a neighborhood of settlers and hence not adapted to establishing the Germans in a colony by themselves in order to preserve their national customs and religion.[55] Solms further states that he was unable to find any proof for the pretended friendship of d'Orvanne with the president and vice-president of Texas, that if there were this relationship between him and the governmental officers of the Texan Republic, it only existed because the Frenchman was connected with "the Verein."

September 1, 1843, the president of Texas had entered under

---
[52] Rosenberg, p. 11. *Entwickelungs-Geschichte*, p. 25. Kordül, p. 259. Kapp, p. 251.
[53] *Jahrbuch für Texas*, 1884; also letter of Solms dated April 27, 1845. These letters will befound in the Original Reports of Solms-Braunfels, quoted *supra*.
[54] Rosenburg, p. 12.
[55] Original Berichte des Prinzen Karl zu Solms in *Deutsch-texanische Monatshefte*, Vol. 9.

contract with Henry F. Fischer and Burchhard Miller under the same conditions as those given to W. S. Peters and others, February 4, 1841. This act had been extended to anyone whom the president in his judgment saw fit to approve.[56] The terms of this contract were: that Fischer and Miller were to introduce 600 families or unmarried men over seventeen years of age; all must be free white settlers of a foreign country; they must settle within three years from date of the contract; the limits of the territory begin at the confluence of the Llano with the Colorado, follow the curves of the Llano to its source, go from there in a direct line 50 English miles south, and from there in a direct line westward to the Colorado and follow the course of the Colorado to the point of beginning. Fischer and Miller were to receive a premium of ten sections for every hundred families, and of five sections for every hundred single men.[57] This contract was raised to number 6,000 families on January 9, 1844.[58] All settlements made by the first of August, 1844, were to be left in possession of the land occupied. Two hundred families (one-third of the required number) had to be brought in by the end of the first year, or the contract became null and void. Every alternate section of land was left in possession of the State.

Fischer travelled to Europe, and under date of June 24, 1844, a contract was signed between Count von Castell, representing the Verein, and Fischer.[59] The Verein promised to pay to Fischer on the same date 100 Friedrich's d'or; on July 5, 1844, $3,600; and on September 1, 1845, $2,000 cash in New Orleans. The Union further promised to raise a capital of $80,000 and to have enough capital by August 1, 1844, to bring in 300 to 400 families. The Union was to receive two-thirds of the profits resulting from sales of land and industrial establishments; Fischer and Miller, one third. The special ex-

---

[56] Hartley's *Digest of Texas Laws*, (2139). Kordül gives the date as Sept. 4, 1843. Kordül, p. 260ff.

[57] This is known as Fischer and Miller's second contract. The first was dated June 7, 1842, but was essentially the same. Rosenberg, p. 12.

[58] *Ibid.*

[59] Kordül, p. 265ff, gives the contract in full.

ecution of colonization was left to a colonial committee of six members, of which Fischer or his appointee was to be one; in this committee, the Verein was to have five votes, Fischer three. For this, the Verein received the rights of Fischer and Miller in the contract. It believed it had really purchased land and hence made the promise of 320 acres to each family, and 160 acres to each unmarried man. The land was 300 miles from the coast and 150 miles from any settlement. It was in the possession of hostile Indian races. Good land could have been bought within the settlements at that time for five to ten cents per acre.[60] They believed on Fischer's word that they could bring out 6,000 families on a capital of $80,000.[61] Soergel, who was on the ground, figured that it would take at least a million dollars to bring over that many colonists.[62] The promises made by the Verein could not possibly have been carried out. This shows the lack of business sense of its members. A little calculation would have shown them that their undertaking was a gigantic affair. If they had received land as they supposed, instead of simply a contract, it still might have been no impossibility as the land might have been sold for some price, and money thus raised.

Solms was friendly received in Texas by the president and members of Congress. The latter considered the presence of the German count in Texas as promising an important immi-

---

[60] Rosenberg, p. 13.
[61] *Entwickelungs-Geschichte*, p. 27.
[62] Soergel, Alwin H., *Für Auswanderungslustige! Briefe eines unter dem Schutze des Mainzer Vereins nach Texas Ausgewanderten*, Leipzig, 1847. Letter under date of April 6, 1846, p. 49. His figures are as follows:

For 2500 persons.

700 wagons @ $80	$56,000
5,600 oxen @ $20 a span	112,000
700 drivers, three months @ $30 per mo.	63,000
3000 oxen advanced to settlers @ $20	60,000
3000 cows @ $8	24,000
1500 horses @ $20	30,000
For 2500 persons. Provisions for 6 mo. @ $20	50,000
Total	$395,000

The purchase of storehouses, surveying, etc., would bring the cost to at least $500,000. For 6000 persons $1,000,000 would not seem too small a sum.

gration of Germans. The count was unfavorably disposed toward Fischer's grant for the reason that he believed that he could obtain from the Texan Congress more favorable terms and a longer contract. He reported to the Directory in Germany that Fischer's grant was too far away in order to carry on trade with Mexico; that it was 80 miles from the plantation of Nassau and 140 miles from the coast; that the Indians still occupied the land and had to be expelled from it.[63] Anson Jones, at that time Secretary of State, informed the prince that the society would obtain from Congress all that it wished at its next session. Had the suggestions of the prince been followed, the future troubles of the colonists might have been avoided.

Their contract was signed June 24, 1844, and by September, 1844, 200 families must be brought over. This was increased to a period of six months longer on January 9, 1844, so the Verein had only eight months and six days with which to fulfill the conditions of the contract. In June, 1844, the Duke of Nassau had been made the protector of the society, Prince von Leiningen, president, Count von Castell, director and vice-president. The members now consisted of twenty-three nobles, of which the Countess zu Isenburg-Meerholz was one.[64] On January 20, 1845, Congress had modified the conditions of Fischer and Miller's contract. They were to have the right to bring over any number of immigrants from 600 to 6,000 and the time was extended to September 1, 1847, within which to fulfill the conditions.[65] In the prospectus of the Verein, it was stated that "not more than one hundred and fifty families would be accepted" the first year, "and not until these have established a sure foundation will a more extensive emigration be encouraged."[66] In November and December, 1844, three ship-loads of emigrants followed Solms-Braunfels who had arrived July first of that year. These were the Bremen barks, "Johann

[63] Berichte des Prinzen Karl zu Solms *Deutsch-texanische Monatshefte*, Vol. 9.
[64] Letter of Prince Solms-Braunfels dated Sophienburg (New Braunfels, Texas), April 27, 1845, quoted in *New Braunfels Zeitung*, May 27, 1870.
[65] Hartley's *Digest*, 2141.
[66] Quoted in Tait's *Edinburgh Magazine* for 1848, p. 220.

Dethard," "Herschel" and "Ferdinand."[67] In the autumn of that year, 110 families and 87 single persons had left Bremen under the auspices of the Union.[68] It is estimated that some 400 German immigrants came to Texas during that year under the protection of the Adelsverein.[69] The Handbuch of the society states that some 200 families, some 700 persons, were sent by the society in September and October, 1844.[70] Another writer says that there were six ships with 496 emigrants sent to Texas in 1844.[71] A rough estimate would be, therefore, that between 400 and 700 persons were brought over by the union during that year. The "Weserzeitung," Bremen, September 25, 1844, says, "that almost never before were seen so many emigrants, among them many persons, who, in accordance with their dress and their many effects, seem to belong to the better class of emigrants. They are the members of the first expedition destined for the colony of the Verein, in Texas. Each ship contained provisions for six months. A physician, surgeon, geometrician, engineer, carpenters, masons, saddlers, bakers, and many apothecaries, accompany the expedition. The ships contain the best kind of surgical instruments, machine parts, etc. Persons are sent to purchase cattle, seeds, etc., in Texas." [72]

From Galveston, the immigrants were shipped on schooners to Lavacca Bay, where a camp was pitched. December 25, of that year, a Christmas festival was given by the prince to the children of the immigrants.[73] The camp was soon removed to Chocolate Bayou, and remained here until all of the colonists had been brought together. It was then pitched at Spring Creek, beyond Victoria. During March, 1845, the prince rode ahead, accompanied by some of his officers, to San Antonio. An old Texan, John Rahm, had told him about "La Fontanas," the beautiful Comal Springs, and upon his advice

---

[67] Letter of Solms-Braunfels as *supra*.
[68] *Der Auswanderer nach Texas*, Bremen, 1846, p. 94.
[69] *Ibid*, p. 94.
[70] *Handbuch*, p. 79.
[71] Büttner, *Briefe*, p. 208, foot-note.
[72] *Weserzeitung*, Sept. 25, 1844; quoted in *Handbuch*, pp. 79-80.
[73] *Jahrbuch für Texas*, pp. 32ff.

he bought from Rafael Garza and his wife, Maria Antonia Veramendi, the Comal tract, March 14, 1845.[74] This tract was a part of Juan Martin's Veramendi estate, which lay fifteen miles above Seguin, surrounding Comal Springs and five miles of the Comal valley. On March 15, 1845, he paid $500 in cash. The purchase price was $1,111 and the balance was to be paid within thirty days.[75] Under the leadership of J. J. von Coll, the immigrants were brought from Victoria[76] and the settlement of the Verein, which afterwards became New Braunfels, was founded.[77] A treaty was made with the Lipan Indians, and the City of New Braunfels, named after the estate of Solms in Germany, was laid out. The first wagons of the immigrants crossed the Guadaloupe March 21, 1845. The town was laid out beside the high steep banks of the Comal river which served as a sort of protection against the Indians. The location for picturesqueness and beauty could not be excelled. "On one side brews the Guadaloupe, while on the other, the beautiful and somewhat inimitable Comal rolls away with its bright crystal waters, with a velocity of some six miles to the hour. As we stood viewing the romantic landscape, our companion, a Virginian, calls out, 'There is nothing like it in the Old Dominion!'"[78] The city lay on a small treeless plain, about half a mile in width and the same distance in length. This plain was bounded on the south by gently sloping hills, on the east by the Guadaloupe, on the north and northwest by the Comal. Beyond the Comal, a steep precipice of some 400 feet or higher descends, which draws away in its northeastern direction to the

---

[74] Seele, Hermann: *A Short History of Comal County, Texas;* New Braunfels, 1885.

[75] *Texas Jahrbuch*, p. 32ff.

[76] Letter dated New Braunfels, May 14, 1845, shows the long period the emigrant had to make this journey. He left Bremen Sept. 23,, 1844, and reached Galveston Nov. 23, 1844. He went from Galveston to Indian Point and remained there two days. On Dec. 5th, he went to Port La Vaca on Mategorda Bay, and remained on shore in tents for two days. Jan. 2, 1845, he moved to Chocolate Creek, seven miles in the interior and waited here four weeks. Then traveled to Victoria and was there three weeks. Moved forty miles into the interior. April 6th, he arrived at last at the settlement. His journey took him seven months. Quoted in Kordül, p. 294.

[77] *History of Comal County.*

[78] *Victoria* (Texas) *Advocate*, Feb. 10, 1847.

other bank of the Guadaloupe. This precipice is covered with a thick forest of red cedars.

The Guadaloupe, which flows east of the town, is a thirty-foot wide stream rushing over a rocky bed. The waters of both the Guadaloupe and the Comal have a purity which scarcely any of the mountain streams of the Alps can equal. Just beyond the city the Guadaloupe unites with the Comal.[79] Prince Solms through his engineers had the town surveyed and laid out in lots.[80] Each of the new immigrants was given a half acre of land in the town, and ten acres in the surrounding country.[81] This was quite different from the promises of 320 and 160 acres respectively. The settlers, however, joyous on account of being freed from their long journey in the wilderness set forth to build their houses, and to regulate their homes.[82] The city was laid out after a regular plan. All streets crossed each other at right angles, and the main streets met in an open square—the market place.[83] A company of twenty men was formed to protect the settlers against the Indians. Hospitals were built, and cannons placed in the city.[84] The Indians, consisting of the Lipans, the Tonkowas and Caranquoes, were treated in a friendly manner by the settlers and the officials of the society. On April 28, 1845, the prince laid the foundations of a stronghold which he called "Sophienburg" after his lady-love.[85]

The expenses of feeding so many people, and the other expenses necessary to carry out so great an undertaking ate up the money of the Verein. The prince was not fitted to carry out such an undertaking. He was a typical noble of a small German State. He had an exaggerated idea of his own importance, and thought he could carry himself in America with the same attitude toward his people as he could in Germany.

---

[79] Roemer, p. 116-117.
[80] *Jahrbuch*, p. 33ff.
[81] Roemer, p. 24.
[82] *Ibid*.
[83] *Ibid*, p. 117.
[84] *Jahrbuch*, p. 32ff.
[85] Letter of Solms quoted above. Letter of Frederick Baare, of Hazleton, Pa., July 13, 1901, says that the fortress was named after the mother of Solms.

He rode around the country followed by a retinue of officers dressed in the fashion of German military officers. His train consisted of an architect, a cook, and a professional hunter (jäger).[86] He would not eat at the same table with others.[87] This did not endear him to the Texan settlers. They, of course, did not understand such conduct. It was entirely out of accord with the free and open life of the plains. He deserves great credit however for the sacrifices which he made, and the efforts he gave to try to better a bad condition of affairs. His greatest lack was, however, his little knowledge of business.[88] The character of the prince is well shown by his signature to the letter of April 27, 1845.[89] The prince was thirty-three years old at the time of his stay in Texas.[90]

The reports of the prince to the colonial directory in Germany show, however, that he understood the conditions of affairs in Texas; that he was active in the interests of the Verein and that he read correctly the motives of such men as Bourgeois d'Orvanne and Fischer. He was evidently a dreamer and thought of establishing in Texas a German State that would gain for the Fatherland all of the commercial advantages which had accrued to England through the East India Company. He understood thoroughly what sort of land was needed to carry out the aims of the Verein and might have obtained it at much more favorable terms, had the German noblemen listened to his re quests.

Fischer had caused the Verein to think that they had enough money to carry out the undertaking. They had not reckoned

---

[86] Cf. *Texas Quarterly*, II, pp. 231-2.

[87] *Ibid*, p. 173.

[88] Cf. Roemer, p. 25. Also Kapp's lecture, *N. Y. Tribune*, Jan. 20, 1855; also Kapp, *Aus und über Amerika*, p. 261ff.

[89] It is signed: Karl Friederich Wilhelm Ludwig Georg Alfred Alexander, Prinz zu Solms, Herr zu Braunfels, Greifenstein, Münzenberg, Wiedenfels, und Sonnenwalde; General Commissaer zum Schutze deutscher Einwanderer in Texas, Sr. Kaiserl, Königl, apostolischen Majestät Rittmeister im König Friedrich August von Sachsen 3. Cuirassier-Regiment, Grosskreuz des königl. Hannoverischen Guelphen-, des Herzogel. Braunschweig'-schen Ordens Heinrichs des Löwen, und Ritter des Ordens von St. Georg von Lucca. Cf. letter quoted *supra*. Letter of F. Baare, June 14, 1909, states that Prince Solms was the half-brother of the later King George of Hanover.

[90] Roemer, *Aus und über Amerika*, Vol. II, p. 260.

on prices in Texas. Prince Solms resigned his position and on February 24, 1845, Baron von Meusebach was appointed his successor.[91] He landed at Galveston in April, 1845, and journeyed from there to Indianola and then to New Braunfels. On his way, he was met by Germans who presented complaints against the society.[92] All writers credit Meusebach with having been a man of great ability. Roemer met him while in Texas and accompanied him on his expedition into the Indian country. Roemer says that the new commissary-general began his activity with the carrying-out of a more regular business policy and a more carefully systematized method of keeping the accounts.[93] Kapp, who visited Texas in the early fifties, says he was a man of heavy calibre and that of all who took part in the undertaking, he was the best educated and the most practical.[94] His real name was Ottfried Hans Freiherr von Meusebach. He was born in the Duchy of Nassau, May 26, 1812. He studied jurisprudence and political science and finance in Bonn and Halle. He had held many offices in Germany before leaving for Texas.[95] His father had been a jurist of high order, and Meusebach himself had been government assessor in Potsdam. He was a diplomatist of great skill. This is shown by his treaty with the Indians and his relations with the Anglo-Americans. He knew how to create respect and obedience. He was looked up to by the Indians. He was unpopular at first with the Germans, but later they came to know his real worth, and in 1852 they chose him as State Senator. He became a naturalized American citizen under the name of John O. Meusebach. He bore himself well under the heaviest stress of circumstances. Kapp says, had he remained in Germany, he would have risen to the highest position.

On May 15, 1845, Solms-Braunfels left, and when von Meusebach entered upon his work, he found affairs at a crisis.

---

[91] *Answer to Interrogatories*, p. 5.
[92] *Fest-Ausgabe*, p. 46.
[93] Roemer, p. 25.
[94] For characerization see Kapp, *Aus und über Amerika*, Vol. II, p. 263ff.
[95] For biography cf. *Fest-Ausgabe*, p. 56. (*Fest-Ausgabe*, hereafter, will be used in place of *Entwickelungs-Geschichte*.)

A number of colonists were on their way to Texas. The money had been spent. As soon as he arrived, he demanded an accounting from the treasurer of the Verein, which that official was unable to give.⁹⁶ The various officers of the society had in the name of the Verein given notes and bills of credit at their own free will. Prince Solms had left for Galveston shortly before the new director's arrival. In that city, Meusebach arranged for a credit of $10,000 and made the prince promise, that, on his arrival in Germany, he would have Count von Castell arrange for a further credit of $20,000. The Verein had promised transportation for $4 per person. It cost the society from $20 to $30 per person. They promised to build houses for $24 and a house could not be built under $100. On his return from Galveston, Meusebach found that some $20,000 ($19,460.02) had been spent by Solms-Braunfels.⁹⁷ In July, 1845, the second lot of immigrants arrived. In a letter dated November 30, 1845, Soergel states that the Verein secretary, Dr. Hill, told him that 2500 persons, in seventeen ships were leaving for Texas.⁹⁸ In a later letter he says that from 5,000 to 6,000 persons are about to emigrate under the auspices of the Verein.⁹⁹ On Meusebach's return, November 1, 1845, he received news that 4,304 emigrants were being sent from Germany. He was in new straits. The treasury was empty, and this large mass of emigrants was about to be thrust upon him. The directory in Germany sent him a credit of $24,000 on a New Orleans banking house. Some 5,000 immigrants were to be landed on the coast and there was only a mere pittance with which to care for them. Meusebach figured the expenses to be about $140,000 to care for and transport the immigrants.¹⁰⁰

---

⁹⁶ *Ibid*, p. 46.
⁹⁷ An account by Meusebach himself will be found in *Answers to Interrogatories*, in case 396, D. C. McCulloch County, Austin, 1894; also cf. *Fest-Ausgabe*, p. 46ff.
⁹⁸ Soergel, A. H. *Für Auswanderungslustige!* Leipzig, 1847, p. 16.
⁹⁹ Letter dated Dec. 5, 1845. *Ibid*, p. 4.
¹⁰⁰ The exact amount is:

    For payment of debt ....$24,000.
    " transportation of 4,304 immigrants 33,161.60
    " support for 3 months @ 10c per day .... 45,000.
    " houses .... 12,000.
    " payment of money advanced by immigrants .. 26,067.

    Total $140,228.60
Cf. *Answers to Interrogatories*.

Germans in Texas 49

By January, 1846, 3,000 persons had landed at Indian Point.[101] From the middle of October, 1845, until the end of April, 1846, thirty-six ships landed at Galveston. Twelve were from Antwerp, and twenty-four from Bremen. These ships landed 5,247 persons.[102] The "Karl Wilhelm" was destroyed and one or two persons lost their lives. Some 2,500 reached New Braunfels and Friedrichsburg. A thousand were left at Indian Point, and on the road towards New Braunfels. Five hundred returned to Germany. Five hundred enlisted in the Mexican war under command of Captain Büchel, about 250 lost their lives at Indian Point, a hundred on the way to the settlements and a hundred on their arrival in New Braunfels.[103] Ervendberg, who was pastor of the German Evangelical Church in New Braunfels, estimates the number who died at about 400.[104] Some had to stay six months along the sandy shore of the bay at Indian Point on account of lack of money. Kapp states the number who died in the summer of 1846, on the way, at New Braunfels and at Friedrichsburg, as 1200.[105] Many of the people had suffered greatly in their trans-atlantic voyage. They were huddled together in the holds, steerage, and on the decks of the ships like sheep, and when they reached shore, they were in a very weak condition. They were covered with vermin. Hundreds died soon after they landed.[106] The condition of affairs became frightful. Some 3,000 were left at Indianola. The shore was covered with improvised tents and huts, chests and coffers, clothing, etc. Roemer says it would remind one of an Oriental caravan.[107] Alwin Soergel was on one of the last ships to enter Galveston, in 1845. He [108] describes his experi-

---

[101] Letter of Jan. 7, 1846 (New Braunfels), in Bracht, p. 227.
[102] Letter of Aug. 9, 1846 (Bracht, p. 243). Roemer says the number was 5246: Roemer, p. 267.
[103] Letter quoted, Bracht, p. 244.
[104] *Ibid.*
[105] Kapp, *Aus und über Amerika*, p. 275.
[106] *Houston Telegraph*, June 19, 1847. This has reference to immigrants of 1846.
[107] Roemer, p. 60.
[108] For accounts of following, cf. Soergel, Alwin H., *Für Auswanderungslustige!* Leipzig, 1847, pp. 21ff. (Soergel was an eye-witness of accounts he narrates); also cf. Kapp, *Aus und über Amerika*, p. 267ff. Based mainly

ences in letters which he wrote home. After a journey of two months, only 2,300 out of 2,500 passengers in all the vessels, entered Galveston. They were then transported to Indian Point. It consisted of a few houses. Barracks of boards were built which afforded refuge for only a few. The rest dwelt in tents. They had to wait more than six months along the low, unhealthy shore. The war with Mexico had taken all means of transportation. The price for transportation rose to enormous sums. There was not enough money among the poor immigrants to purchase teams. Rain and north wind poured through the dwellings. Wood and water were lacking. They were surrounded by swamps in which mosquitoes swarmed, and fevers arose. Rum holes increased their misery and changed men into beasts. Many fell a prey to epidemics.[109] The summer broke out with its terrible heat. Whole families betook themselves on the road to New Braunfels. The whole road was lined with corpses of dead or with dying men. In many instances the settlers along the way were forced to bury the bodies of immigrants who had been left by their companions to die by the wayside unpitied and alone.[110] Wolves and vultures followed them along their routes. In the day was heard the cry of beasts of prey; in the night, the howl of wolves and the shrill cry of the Comanches. One man left his wife to perish and later was left by his companions. Arrived in New Braunfels, conditions became worse. The place was without means of sustenance. The poor peasants tried to forget their misery by dancing and drinking. It is even stated that men were torn from their wives and buried before they were dead.[111] All human ties were broken. This was the condition of affairs that von Meusebach had to face. In the summer of '46, there were still several hundred persons camping on the coast. Things changed. The last immi-

---

on Soergel; also, article by H. Seele in *Texas Jahrbuch* for 1884; Eickhoff, *In der Neuen Heimath*, p. 327ff; also *N. Y. Tribune*, Jan. 20, 1855; *Houston Telegraph*, June 19, 1847, article entitled, Emigrants of 1846. All are substantially the same. Kapp says this condition was no exaggeration. He was in the colony in 1852.

[109] Kapp says two-thirds died of epidemic. Soergel says one-third.
[110] This is the statement of the *Houston Telegraph*, June 19, 1847.
[111] This was in Friedrichsburg.

grant was brought to New Braunfels. Camps were pitched on both sides of the Comal and Guadaloupe rivers. Horses, oxen and cattle grazed beside hut or tent.

In March, 1846, Meusebach raised money on credit, and arranged for the transportation of the immigrants. In the middle of December, '45, he sent thirty-six men to break a way north of the Pedernales. In the beginning of 1846, block-houses were built. This became the later settlement of Friedrichsburg. On April 23, 1846, the first settlers were sent thither. They consisted of about twelve persons.[112] On Friday, May 8, 1846, they reached their new home. As soon as possible the commissioner-general sent hither the new arrivals from Germany. He became acquainted with a certain Dr. Schubert and placed him in command of the new settlement. Schubert built here a wretched inn and made a journey to the limits of the land. This was in the territory of the Comanche Indians. In April, Meusebach betook himself to the Farm "Nassau" to obtain grain and supplies for the people in Indianola and New Braunfels but without any result.[113] The Verein representative in Galveston, von Kläner, was informed of the condition of affairs. He wrote to Germany, and $60,000 was sent September 7, 1846, to the administrator of the Verein, in Texas.[114] With this, the condition of affairs was changed for the better. Friedrichsburg numbered 1,000 souls by August, 1846.[115] The danger from the Comanches caused Meusebach to go himself, January, 1847, from Friedrichsburg to the Llano river. He signed a treaty with the Indians.[116] Ferdinand Roemer, the scientist, accompanied him on this expedition.[117] Meusebach had, previously to this expedition, given his resignation. He gave up his office July 20, 1847, after his three months' expedition among the Indians was completed.[118] During the winter of 1845, the Ger-

---

[112] *Fest-Ausgabe*, p. 50.
[113] *Ibid*, p. 60ff.
[114] Rosenberg, p. 19.
[115] *Fest-Ausgabe*, p. 51.
[116] Letter of Bracht, Aug. 9, 1846, p. 243.
[117] Cf. account in *Houston Telegraph*, May 10, 1847.
[118] Cf. Roemer's account, Roemer, Ch. 18 and 19.

man Protestant Society built the first church out of cedar wood. This was dedicated March 22, 1846. This society was the first German protestant association and the first incorporated company in Comal county.[119]

H. Spies became Meusebach's successor in office as director general. Spies and Dr. Herff had arranged a special contract with the Verein for the settlement of a new colony. They paid the Verein 30,000 gulden ($12,000).[120] During Meusebach's administration, the small settlements of Castell, Leiningen and Meerholz, on the Llano river, were founded. Castell is to-day quite a settlement. Leiningen is a small settlement. Meerholz has disappeared.[121] The so-called "Darmstaedter" settlement was laid out on the north bank of the Llano under the administration of Spies. It was a communistic colony, and was named "Bettina" after the author, Bettina von Arnim.[122] Besides Spies, G. Dresel was made general business agent of the society. He had charge of the finances of the society.[123] Spies had the idea that Schubert (his real name was Struberg) wished to obtain the "Farm Nassau" by force. A combat ensued in which a man was killed. Spies and his confederates were tried for murder. This cost the Verein a large amount.[124] On March 2, 1850, the "Gesangverein Germania" was established. Under its auspices, the first public holiday was celebrated July 4, of that year.[125] The New Braunfels "Zeitung" was established under the editorship of Ferdinand Lindheimer, and its first number appeared November 12, 1852.[126] During the same year, Spies was succeeded by L. Bene.[127] The inhabitants of New Braunfels were in dispute over the title to their lands. The first number of the "Zeitung" contained a call of a

---

[119] *Fest-Ausgabe*, p. 52.
[120] *Fest-Ausgabe*, p. 52.
[121] Rosenberg, p. 20.
[122] Cf. account, *The Communistic Colony of Bettina, Texas Hist. Quarterly*, III, 33.
[123] *Fest-Ausgabe*, p. 53.
[124] *Ibid*.
[125] *Jahrbuch* as *supra*.
[126] *Ibid*.
[127] Rosenberg, p. 22.

committee of citizens to defend their rights against the Bastrop claimants and other separate claims.[128] By 1853, the Verein gave up all its relations in Texas. Bene had sold the Farm Nassau for $15,000 to Otto von Roeder. Later, the farm was sold for $500 to cover a Verein debt. Roeder lost all.[129] The Verein had measured 4,500 square miles of land at a cost of $80,000. Half of this was reserved for the State. The Union lost possession of all its lands. In 1855, Fischer had gone to Europe and had persuaded the people that he could bring affairs into a flourishing condition again. He was appointed general agent of the society and was recognized as such by the Texan government.[130] His first official act was an attempt, June 15, 1857, to legalize the suspended "Headrights" which had been given up by the legislature of 1852.

The Verein had great difficulty in maintaining its rights to the land grants which it had received, both from the Texan Republic and from the government of the State of Texas. The commissioners appointed by the latter issued grants of 1,735,200 acres to the Verein. Fischer and Miller had assigned on December 30, 1845, its principal interest in the contract to the German Emigration Society, as the Verein was officially designated by the Texan government.

The expenses of the enterprise were enormous. The surveys cost the Society alone $120,000. The Society became badly in debt and the legislature of Texas passed a law Jan. 21, 1850, declaring that creditors of the company should have a lien, in the nature of a mortgage, upon the premium lands of the company. The company was permitted to receive its share of the land direct from the state.

On September 15, 1853, the company assigned and transferred to their Texan creditors all their property in Texas and all rights accruing to them by the colonization contract. After the creditors had thus gained the land from the Verein, the legislature took it from the former and granted it to the colonists or their assignees. (Statutes of Texas Vol. 5.)

---

[128] *Jahrbuch* as *supra*.
[129] Rosenberg, p. 23.
[130] Rosenberg, p. 22.

During the year 1847, 8,000 Germans landed at the port of Galveston, and during three months previous to July, 1847, 4,020 Germans had landed at that port.[181]

In April, 1848, there was founded at Biebrich, the "Deutsche Colonisationsgesellschaft für Texas."[132] The Graf von Castell was made president of this society. A certain Ludwig Martin was the moving spirit. He says that the members consisted of himself, whom he styles advocate of Freiburg, Graf von Castell, and railroad director, Ubaghs. It offered roseate promises similar to those of the "Adelsverein," if that were possible.[133] It offered for a capital of $280, 100 acres of land in Bexar County, or along the coast, including a log house; also a herd of cattle so that the possessor could begin his labor immediately. Fifty dollars was to be paid in Germany; $100 in the grant, and the rest on time. An agent was to accompany the emigrant to the place of abode. This came to naught, and simply shows that the idea of the Verein still held root.

After the catastrophe of the Adelsverein, emigration stopped until the Revolution of '48. High officers, State officials, aristocrats, teachers, merchants and peasants came in great numbers.[134] Besides the singing society, numerous societies were formed. The colony now became flourishing. Mills were established, and the industrious German people soon forgot the troubles of the forties.

> "Und haben sie hier nicht Veilchen duft,
> Sie haben doch Rosen zu schenken,—
> Und texanische Luft ist freie Luft
> Das wollen wir freudig bedenken."[135]

---

[131] Löher, p. 273.

[132] Cf. Roemer, p. 230.

[133] Martin, Ludwig: *Der nord amerikanische Freistaat Texas, ein Handbuch für solche, die dahin inbesondere aber nach dem der deutschen Colonisationsgesellschaft für Texas angehörigen, in der County Bexar gelegenen Land bezirk auswandern wollen. von Ludwig Martin, Landbesitzer im Staate Texas und Mitglied der deutschen Colonisationsgesellschaft für Texas.* Wiesbaden, 1848.

[134] Mgebroff, pp. 1-7.

[135] Nies, Conrad, *Aus westlichen Weiten*, Leipzig, 1905.

CHAPTER IV.

NUMBERS OF GERMANS IN TEXAS. INDUSTRIES, COTTON CULTURE, WAGES, CHARACTER AND METHOD OF LIFE, COMPARISON AND RELATIONS WITH THE AMERICANS.

POPULATION.

It is difficult to state definitely how many Germans have immigrated to Texas. During the great Galveston flood of 1900, all reports of the Custom House were lost for the years 1840-1860. It is hard to sift from newspaper accounts, and those of travellers, the exact number of those immigrating. It is also difficult to state the number, because many were landed at New Orleans and some of these may have gone overland to Texas. To-day, 1907, the German population of Southern and Southwestern Texas is estimated to be between seventy-five and one hundred thousand.[1] The population of Western Texas, since the great immigration of the forties, has always been mainly of German extraction. The Germans there have kept their identity as a race. The German language is the most commonly spoken. German customs of life still hold sway. The German Sangverein still exerts a strong influence, and one would see there, probably, the most thoroughly Germanized portion of the United States. This is due to several reasons. The Germans were the earliest settlers in those districts. They all settled at one point. They came in such great numbers that they were able to populate whole counties. Comal and Gillespie Counties to-day are almost entirely German in sentiment, in speech, and in methods of life. Another reason why the German element has not been merged into that of the American, is because so many of them were educated men, and were able to become leaders in the community. During the fifties, the known antipathy of the Germans to slave labor and the competition between slave and free labor, kept the

---

[1] *The Passing Show*, San Antonio, February 23, 1907.

Anglo-Americans from settling in the neighborhood. This was not true of the northern states. The well edited German newspapers such as the *San Antonio Zeitung* and *New Braunfels Zeitung,* edited by such men as Dr. Adolf Douai and Dr. Ferdinand Lindheimer, also exerted an immense influence.

That the German element was strong in the early forties has been shown in preceding chapters. That there were many Germans in Texas in the thirties has also been shown. They numbered several hundred and were situated in the small towns in the vicinity of Industry. They came mainly from the Duchy of Oldenburg, and were induced to settle in Texas through the letter of Fritz Ernst.[2] Many settlements had been formed as has been previously shown. A writer states in 1840, that of all European races the Germans are always in the majority.[3] Another[4] says, that in a few years, the Germans will be as strong and as numerous as the Americans. He estimates the population of Texas in 1841, as follows:—

Spanish and Mexicans	8,000
North Americans	130,000
English	20,000
Germans	10,000
French	15,000 [5]
Scotch	10,000
Irish	12,000
Negroes	45,000

If his statements are true, the Germans had almost one-tenth as many as the Americans. In the early forties, the newspapers were filled with accounts of Germans arriving in Galveston and Houston. The *Weser Zeitung* gives the following as the number departing for Galveston from Bremen:—[6]

---

[2] Cf. Ch. II, *supra.*
[3] Hoehne, Friedrich, *Wahn und Überzeugung,* etc. Weimar, 1844, p. 187. Letter dated January, 1840.
[4] Kordül, p. 80 (footnote).
[5] The French were probably in the eastern part near to Louisiana.
[6] Quoted in *Der Auswanderer nach Texas,* Bremen, 1846, p. 9.

1842— 77 passengers in three ships.
1843— 66 " " five "
1844— 496 " " six "
1845—3,134 " " 22 "
Total 3,773 passengers in 36 ships.

It gives the number departing for New Orleans, as follows:—

1841—2,067 passengers in 15 ships.
1842—3,850 " " 26 "
1843—3,281 " " 22 "
1844—6,001 " " 35 "
1845—9,626 " " 56 "
Total 24,825 passengers in 154 ships.

It further states that a large number of the passengers sailing for New Orleans are supposed to have gone to Texas.

Lorenzo Castro brought over from Alsace and Lorraine from 1842 to 1847 5,200 in twenty-seven ships.[7] A large majority was French, but without doubt many Germans were among them. Froebel, who visited the colony, said that he was surprised that they called themselves Germans.[8]

In 1839, 40 families of Germans landed in Texas, and 400 families were said to be coming before January, 1840.[9] On January 7, 1843, 117 immigrants are reported as having arrived at Galveston.[10] Sixty families arrived by February 1, 1843.[11] The same paper notes the arrival of 52 and 129 immigrants under date of December 27, 1843, and January 17, 1844, respectively. During the year 1844, two ships, the "Ferdinand" and "Herschel", brought over some 700 persons. They had been preceded by the "Johann Dethard", which brought over the first passengers under the auspices of the "Verein".[12] From the middle of October, 1845, up to April, 1846, 5,247 Germans landed in

---

[7] Castro, Lorenzo, *Immigration from Alsace and Lorraine.* New York, 1871.
[8] Froebel, Central America, London, 1859, p. 423.
[9] *Houston Telegraph,* December 11, 1839.
[10] *Civilian and Galveston Gazette,* January 7, 1843.
[11] *Houston Telegraph,* February 1, 1843.
[12] *Fest-Ausgabe,* p. 39

Texas under the auspices of the "Adelsverein".[13] Three thousand immigrants were at Indian Point, Feb. 2, 1846.[14] New Braunfels by May 14, 1845, had a population of 1500. It contained 300 wooden houses. There were one retail store, six groceries, a silversmith, a coppersmith, a locksmith, a saddler, six shoemakers, four furniture dealers, two tanners, three cigar factories, a wagon maker, three blacksmiths and a bakery.[15] Galveston in 1846 is said to have had a population of 4,000, of which one-half were Germans.[16] In January, 1846, New Braunfels is described as having 150 dwelling houses; a population made up of 800 Germans, 100 Texan Germans, 50 Americans, 12 Mexicans, and some of the members of Castro's colony.[17] By October of that year, that town had increased to 2500 domiciled settlers, although there were three thousand persons living there.[18] By March of the following year, it had grown to 3,000 inhabitants, and Fredericksburg had more than a thousand persons.[19] The latter place by April had increased to 1,100 and contained two stores and some 150 block houses.[20]

According to Franz Löher, 7,161 Germans landed at Galveston alone during the years 1841-1846, and 8,000 landed at that port during the year 1847.[21] According to Soergel, there were some six to seven thousand living in Galveston, Houston, Mill Creek, Indian Point, Victoria, New Braunfels and Castel.[22] The *Houston Telegraph* states that under the auspices of the "Verein", some 6,000 immigrants have been brought, up to the year 1847, to this country; that their settlements extended from the coast to the territory of the Comanches.[23] Löher [24] says, that

---

[13] Bracht, p. 244.
[14] *Neuste Briefe und Nachrichten aus Texas*, Heilbron, 1846, p. 12.
[15] Letter May 14, 1845. Kordül, p. 367.
[16] Sommer, p. 9. Letter dated Galveston, June 6, 1846.
[17] Bracht, p. 234. Letter dated January 11, 1846.
[18] *Ibid*, p. 254.
[19] Letter March 13, 1847. Bracht, p. 258.
[20] Letter April 28, 1847. *Ibid*, p. 266.
[21] Löher, Franz, pp. 272-273.
[22] Soergel, *Neuste Nachrichten*. Eisleben, 1847, pp. 21-31.
[23] *Houston Telegraph*, October 28, 1847.
[24] Löher, p. 353.

there were 150,000 whites in Texas, 30,000 of whom were Germans. This cannot be far from right as the Census of 1850 gives the number of whites as 154,034. The number of Germans stated must be approximately correct, as the *New York Tribune* for 1856 [25] gives the number of Germans as 20,000, and other writers state that the number was 30,000.[26] This made the number of Germans as one-fifth of the white population. Wisconsin, according to Löher's statistics, had a German population of two-fifths. Missouri had one-fifth; Virginia, Delaware and Maryland each one-fourth. The German element in Texas, however, was more compact than in any of the other states, excepting, perhaps, Wisconsin, and hence was bound to exert more of an influence, especially in sparsely settled communities such as Texas was made up of. Von Behr, writing before 1847, says that Galveston was more than one-half German, and that the "Verein" colony contains about 10,000 inhabitants.[27] Bracht estimates the number of Germans in 1849 from Germany in Texas, as 15,000, and 10,000 to 15,000 from the United States. The white population, estimated at that time by the number of voters in the various counties, was 137,931.[28] This would make the Germans number one-sixth of the white population. He further states that one-tenth of the white population three years before (1845 or 1846) was German.[29] He divides the population of the Germans as follows:—10,000 west of the Colorado; 6,000 in the neighborhood between the Colorado and Brazos; 5,000 in Galveston and Houston; and the rest scattered.[30]

The newspapers are filled with accounts of the arrival of German immigrants. By December 7, 1848, 130 reached Houston. They were all provided with comforts.[31] That winter twelve hundred were expected under the auspices of the "Verein". This

---

[25] Bruncken, *German Political Refugees*, p. 58.
[26] Adolf Douai says the Mainzerverein colonized Texas with 30,000 Germans. He was editor for years of the *San Antonio Zeitung*. Douai, *Land und Leute*. Berlin, 1864, p. 329.
[27] Von Behr, Ottomar, 1847, p. 88.
[28] Bracht, pp. 99-101.
[29] *Ibid*, p. 103.
[30] *Ibid*.
[31] *Houston Telegraph*, December 7, 1848.

was stated by an agent of that Society.[32] A year later, 300 had arrived in Texas.[33] These were mainly those departing on account of the Revolution of '48. Many of them were wealthy, and the majority was in comfortable circumstances.[34]

About 100 immigrants arrived at Houston in 1850. They proceeded immediately to the interior, and settled at Mill Creek, New Braunfels and Fredericksburg.[35] During that year several thousand immigrants were said to be on their way to Texas.[36] The following vessels from Bremen were on their way to Galveston:—[37]

"Eslafette", D. H. Heyer............Sept. 15.
"Paquese", Buenos Ayres............ "   "
"Solon", Ballehr................... "   16.
"Magnet", Hasloop .... "   "
"Hermann", Theodor, B. F. Müller....Oct. 1.
"Reform", Amerman.................   "   "
Another vessel, name not given........ " 15.

From Hamburg, bound for Galveston, came the ship "Bremen", with immigrants, and the bark "Alex".

In 1847-8, Fredericksburg had 2,000 inhabitants, Comal City 250, Leiningen 140, Victoria 1200, Castroville 700, Dhannies 200, Industry 200, Indian Point 250.[38] The majority of the population in all these places was German. In 1852 Galveston had a population of 7,000, of which one-fourth was German.[39] Before 1853 New Braunfels had 3,000 and Indianola 1,000.[40]

The *Deutsche Gesellschaft* of New Orleans aided many Germans to go to Texas. In order to get an idea of how many Germans came to Texas by way of New Orleans, and how many did not come from Germany direct to Texas, the following statistics are given—there were sent to Texas by that society:

---

[32] Victoria, Texas, *Advocate*, August 31, 1848.
[33] *Mercantile Advertiser* (Houston), December 8 and 15, 1849.
[34] *Ibid*, December 15, 1849.
[35] *Houston Telegraph*, December 6, 1850.
[36] *Ibid*, October 30, 1850.
[37] *Ibid*.
[38] Bracht, p. 213.
[39] Article by Kapp, May 19, 1852, *Atlantische Studien*, Vol. I. p. 173.
[40] Büttner, *Briefe*, Bamberg, 1853.

In 1847-8, 317 immigrants.
" 1848-9, 277 "
" 1849-50, 86 "
" 1850-1, 366 "
" 1851-2, 1,209 "
" 1852-3, 1,504 "
" 1853-4, 1,566 "
" 1854-5, 1,290 "
" 1855-6, 190 "
" 1856-7, 417 "
" 1857-8, 111 "
" 1859-60, 63 "
" 1860-1, 238 "

Total, 7,634 "

There were none during the Civil War. Beginning with 1865, the following number of Germans were sent through the auspices of the society to Texas:—

In 1865-6, 25 immigrants.
" 1866-7, 16 "
" 1867-8, 270 "
" 1868-9, 306 "
" 1869-70, 893 "
" 1870-1, 1,361 "
" 1871-2, 1,876 "
" 1873-4, 1,933 "
" 1874-5, 746 "
" 1875-6, 717 "
" 1876-7, 590 "
" 1877-8, 598 "
" 1878-9, 561 "
" 1879-80, 1,006 "
" 1880-1, 1,228 "
" 1881-2, 678 "
" 1882-3, 600 "
" 1883-4, 300 "
" 1884-5, 250 "
" 1885-6, 250 " 41

Total, 14,204 " 41

It is noticeable that the immigration to New Orleans before 1852-3 is small in comparison with the following years. This is due probably to the fact that the Germans were sent direct to

[41] Deiler, Hanno, *Geschichte der deutschen Gesellschaft von New Orleans*, 1897, p. 54ff. These statistics are taken from the books of the Society.

Galveston or Indianola in the ships of the "Mainzverein". After 1853, the "Verein" withdrew from Texas, and so the immigration came via New Orleans.

The Census of 1850 [42] in giving its estimate of the number of Germans in Texas is very far from the truth. It gives 8,191 as having their birth place in Germany. The whole white population was 154,034. The same year Wisconsin had 191,881 and Missouri 592,004 whites. San Antonio, Texas, in 1856 [43] alone had 3,000 Germans and Galveston in 1852 about 2,000.[44] There were 5,000 Germans in the vicinity of Houston. This was shown by a Census taken in 1857.[45] In 1857, 10,000 Germans are reported to have departed from the Duchy of Mecklenberg-Schwerin alone.[46] Western Texas had 25,000 Germans in 1857.[47] If we take 30,000 as being approximately correct, it will be seen that Texas had one-fifth of its population composed of Germans. Wisconsin had 191,881 whites, of whom 34,519 were Germans, or a little over one-sixth; Missouri, 592,004 whites, of whom 44,352 were Germans, or seven and one-half per cent. The statistics for Wisconsin and Missouri are probably more accurate than those of Texas. Kapp stated the proportion in Texas to be two-fifths native Americans, two-fifths of German origin and one-fifth Mexican. This is a rather large proportion. Olmsted [48] gives the following statement regarding the German population:

"There are estimated to be at the commencement of 1857, 35,000 Germans in Texas, of whom about 25,000 are settled in the German and half-German colonies of Western Texas."

In a footnote he states: [49]

"In Comal, Gillespie and Medina Counties, nearly all the inhabitants are Germans. In Victoria and Colorado Counties they constitute about three-fourths of the population; in Calhoun, Bastrop and Bexar (excluding San Antonio) about one-half; in Fayette, Caldwell, Travis and San Antonio City about one-third, and in

---

[42] *Census of 1850.*
[43] Olmsted, *Texas Journeys*, p. 160.
[44] *Atlantische Studien*, Vol. I, p. 173.
[45] *Houston Telegraph*, June 14, 1857.
[46] *San Antonio Ledger*, September 26, 1857.
[47] Olmsted, *Texas Journeys*, p. 441.
[48] *Ibid*, p. 428.
[49] *Ibid*, footnote.

Hays about one-fourth. I have from an intelligent source, the following estimate by counties, with a larger footing. The Census of 1850 is thought to be of little value in respect to reports upon the nativities of Texans.

"Eastern Texas: Galveston, 3500; Houston, 3000; Harris County, 1000; scattered, 1000; total, 8500.

"Central Texas: Austin, 3000; Washington, 1000; Travis, 2000; Colorado, 1200; Bastrop, 1100; Fayette, 1000; Milam, 500; other counties, 400; total, 10,200 (part west of Colorado).

"Western Texas: Comal, 3500; Gillespie, 2000; Bexar, 5000; Medina, 1500; Guadaloupe, 1500; Victoria, 1500; Dewitt, 1500; Calhoun, 1200; Karnes, 800; Caldwell, 400; Nueces, 400; Llano, 400; Hayes, 300; Karr, 300; Gonzales, 300; Rio Grande Cos., 1100; total, 21,700. Total in State, 40,400."[50]

The above statistics prepare us to accept the statements of Kapp, Olmsted, Roemer, and others, that the Germans of Texas formed a more important part of the population than in any other southern state.[51] Bruncken goes so far as to state that in no state did the Germans form as important a part of the population as in Texas.[52] Kapp says that, "although this number is but small comparatively speaking, German manners and German mind have more influence and are more respected than anywhere else in the United States. The reason is, that the German elements appear there as the first pioneers of the civilization, and sustain that character.[53] Roemer says: "Next to the Anglo-Americans, the Germans form by far the most important part of the population."[54] Olmsted states that "on entering Texas, we had been so ignorant as not to know that there were larger settlements there than in any other southern state."[55]

What about the German population after the fifties? Did it keep up its proportion? By the Census of 1860 Texas had 20,553 persons born in Germany, out of a white population of 377,893; Wisconsin, 123,879, out of a white population of 773,-693; and Missouri, 88,487, out of a white population of 1,063,-

---

[50] *Bibliothèque Universale de Genéve*, Vol. 35, p. 303, gives the same number as Olmsted. It is evidently based upon Olmsted.

[51] Olmsted, p. 132. Roemer, p. 59. Kapp's lecture, *N. Y. Tribune*, January 20, 1855.

[52] Bruncken, *Political Refugees*, p. 58. 1904.

[53] *N. Y. Tribune*, January 20, 1855.

[54] Roemer, p. 59. This refers to Galveston.

[55] Olmsted, *Texas Journeys*, p. 152.

64   *Germans in Texas*

489. This is evidently, also, inaccurate. Census of 1870: Texas, white population, 564,700, German, 23,985; Wisconsin, white population, 1,051,351, German, 162,314; Missouri, white population, 1,603,146, German 113,618. This, as in the Census of 1850 and that of 1860, is not correct as far as Texas is concerned. The districts of Germany represented in Texas, according to the Census of 1870 are:

> Baden—686
> Bavaria—837
> Brunswick—411
> Hamburg—140
> Hannover—1,525
> Hessen—1,065
> Lubeck—2
> Mecklenberg—466 [56]
> Nassau—477 [56]
> Oldenburg—475 [57]
> Prussia—13,781.

According to King, who visited Texas in 1873 and 1874, New Braunfels had a population of 4,000; Comal County, in which New Braunfels is situated, probably 10,000. He states that New Braunfels bears as many evidences of wealth and prosperity as any town in the Middle States.

In 1900, there were in Texas 48,295 persons who were born in Germany, and 157,214 who had either a father or a mother born in Germany.[58]

Goegg, who travelled through Texas sometime before 1883, states that Galveston at that time had 40,000 inhabitants;[59] San Antonio,[60] 20,000, of whom 8,000 were Germans; Austin,[61] 20,000, one-third of whom were Germans; Brenham,[62] 6,000, three-fourths of whom were Germans; Dallas,[63] 17,000, two-

---

[56] These amounts are wrong on their face, as the headquarters of the Verein was Nassau.

[57] There were probably that many, in the early forties, from the Duchy of Oldenburg alone.

[58] *Monatsbuch für Texas*, 1904; also *Census of U. S.*, 1900.

[59] One-fourth of whom were Germans. *Ibid*, p. 126.

[60] Goegg, Amand, *Ueberseeische Reisen*, Zurich, 1888.

[61] *Ibid*, p. 137.

[62] *Ibid*, p. 138.

[63] *Ibid*, p. 139.

thirds of whom were Germans; Fredericksburg, 2,000, all of whom were Germans.[64]

In 1904, the majority of the German population lived in Gillespie, Kendall, Comal and Bexar Counties. Fredericksburg was entirely German. San Antonio contained 60,000 inhabitants, of whom one-third were Germans. It is interesting to note that many of the Mexicans and negroes of San Antonio understood German. There were, in 1904, 22,384 German farmer families in Texas.[65]

Recently there has been formed a league of the different German societies in Texas. In a way, it may be styled a successor to the "Adelsverein". It was organized in November, 1906, at Houston, Texas. It has already 800 members, and is growing rapidly. It is known as the "German Immigration League of Texas". The officers of the League are George P. Zeiss, of Houston, president; Friedrich Hofheinz, of New Braunfels, first vice-president, and M. Tillig, of Houston, secretary. The various German societies of Texas are joining the league in a body. The league begins its work in March of this year (1907) by publishing 100,000 pamphlets descriptive of Texas and its industries. These are to be sent to Germany. The president is to go in July of this year (1907) to Germany to lecture on Texas, besides advertising by other methods. That German immigration will be increased is expected.[66]

INDUSTRIES.

The Germans have always been famed for their industry. It was as true in Texas as it was in the Fatherland. Probably no settlements in the South of similar size could show as many varied industries as the small German settlements of Western Texas. The immigrants settling in that district of the State were able to keep their racial identity. The skilled workman of Germany was able to continue his trade on coming to Texas. What town in the South of like size could show as many different industries previous to the Civil War as New Braunfels after its

---

[64] *Ibid*, p. 142.
[65] This paragraph is based on *Handbuch des Deuchthums im Auslande*, Berlin, 1904, pp. 116-117.
[66] The *Passing Show*, San Antonio, Texas, February 23, 1907.

first year of settlement? It had in 1845 one retail store, three groceries, a silversmith, a coppersmith, a saddler, six shoemakers, four cabinetmakers, a wagon maker, a locksmith, two tanneries, three cigar factories, a bakery, and a house painter. The "Verein" had two civil engineers in its employ.[67] That association brought over several druggists, physicians, etc. The majority of the population at first as to-day, was engaged in agriculture. To-day there are said to be 22,384 German farmer families in Texas.[68] Farming was carried on on a small scale. As in Germany, intensive agriculture was used in Texas. This resulted partly from the fact that the "Verein" gave each settler ten acres of land. Olmsted describes the farms about New Braunfels as follows:

"They lived in little log cabins, and had inclosures of ten acres of land about them. * * * The greater variety of the crops which had been grown upon their allotments, and the more clean and complete tillage they had received contrasted favorably with the patches of corn-stubble, overgrown with crab-grass, which are usually the only gardens to be seen adjoining the cabins of the poor whites and slaves. The people themselves were also to be seen, men, women and children, busy at some work."[69]

The nobles as well as the peasants engaged in an industry of some kind. In the early forties, men like the von Roeders were farmers, Robert Justus Kleberg, Sr., who had held important positions in Germany, at one time made cigars.[70] Count Henckel von Donnersmark kept the first grocery in New Braunfels.[71] Roemer says regarding him:

"The other wooden building was the inn of the place, also at the same time mercantile house and hostelry. Its owner is a young German count, H. v. D., who earlier an ensign in the Prussian army, had immigrated to Texas under Prince Solms the year before my arrival and had developed such a practical, worldly wisdom and activity for the foundation of his external welfare, that he had gained in less than a course of a year many thousands of dollars. * * * The inn, to which he especially thanks his fortunate financial condition, took its origin from the most unimportant be-

[67] Letter May 14, 1845. *Kordül*, pp. 306-307.
[68] *Cf.* Note 65, *supra.*
[69] Olmsted, *Texas Journeys*, p. 140.
[70] *Cf.* Ch. II, *supra.*
[71] *San Antonio Express*, October 4, 1903.

ginnings, as he at the time of the founding of the city sold by draught brandy bought at San Antonio by the barrel.[72] Baron Wedemeyer, son of the Prime Minister to the King of Hanover, ran a farm. Beer and wine were dispensed by Baron Kriewiez von Zypry, from Berlin, who lived among the Indians several years.[73] Baron von Nauendorf sold liquors. Baron von Dalbigh was a 'cowboy.'[74] Officers, counts, barons, noblemen, are seen here metamorphosed as ox-drivers, farmers and servants. * * * A Herr von C., who had earlier eaten at the royal table in the Hanoverian court, was engaged as a Texan postillion."[75]

In 1847, a letter from New Braunfels states that mechanics and laboring men of all kinds are very busy and are well paid and many such will find good opportunities and business as well as a good support for life.[76] The place at that time had two apothecaries, two physicians, several bakeries, and a beer brewery.[77] As early as 1845 the majority of the hand workers and retailers of Galveston were composed of Germans.[78] An increasing number of mercantile pursuits were being occupied by men of that race.[79] It is declared that the Germans were so industrious that "they over-observed the 4th Commandment, and not only worked six days, but refused to rest on the Sabbath".[80] The *Texas State Gazette* declares in 1855:

"Where they have settled in any considerable number, the country around them looks more thriving and flourishing than in most other portions; so we say again let them come, there is room enough, and they will be made welcome."[81]

In 1857 New Braunfels contained fifteen drygoods and grocery stores, two drug stores, four hotels, eleven boarding houses, two theaters, one billiard saloon, ten blacksmith shops, two locksmiths, two gunsmiths, one printing office, one library,

---

[72] Roemer, p. 122. This was in 1846.
[73] *San Antonio Express*, October 4, 1903.
[74] *The Passing Show*, San Antonio, February 23, 1907.
[75] *Atlantische Studien*, Vol. VI, p. 20.
[76] *Galveston Weekly News*, March 20, 1847; quoted in Bracht, p. 139.
[77] *Ibid.*
[78] Roemer, p. 59.
[79] *Ibid.*
[80] *Southern Intelligencer*, May 27, 1857.
[81] *Texas State Gazette*, Austin, June 30, 1855.

thirteen carpenters, thirteen stonemasons, five tanners, five bakeries, two brick and lime kilns, fifteen cabinetmakers, two upholsterers, four butchers, five wagon makers, one carriage factory, two nurseries, three ten pin alleys, five saddler shops, two jewelers, a great many tailors, three shoemakers, three doctors, and mechanics of almost every kind.[82]

"The town population which consists mostly of Germans, taken altogether is perhaps the most quiet, peaceable and industrious community in this or any other state in the Union." [83] According to Olmsted, in 1856, there were seven wagon manufactories in New Braunfels. The Germans were said to make better wagons than the Americans.

There were four grist mills in New Braunfels when Olmsted visited the town, a sash and blind factory was being erected, and a cotton factory was contemplated.[85] He states that half the population is composed of agricultural laborers, or farmers, who themselves follow the plough.[86] He gives the following as the number of mechanics and laborers:

Carpenters and builders	20
Wagon makers	8
Gun and Locksmiths	2
Coppersmiths	2
Machinists	2
Saddlers	3
Shoemakers	6
Turners	2
Tailors	5
Button and fringe makers	1
Tanners	3
Butchers	3
Bakers	4

---

[82] *Southern Intelligencer,* June 3, 1857.
[83] *Ibid.*
[84] Olmsted, p. 142.
[85] Olmsted, *Texas Journeys,* p. 178.
[86] *Ibid,* p. 177.

He says that he does not "think that there is another town in the slave states in which the proportion to the whole population of mechanics, or of persons employed in the exercise of their own discretion in productive occupations, is one-quarter as large as in New Braunfels, unless it be some other in which the Germans are the predominating race." [87]

In 1858 a large manufacturing establishment was established at New Braunfels for the making of coarse fabrics.[88] The Comal river had quite a rapid current, and it furnished fine water power. It had a rocky bed and this made quite a falls near the town of New Braunfels. Most of the factories erected were run by water power.

The Counties of Comal and Gillespie are almost entirely composed of Germans. According to the Census of 1860, Comal had sixteen establishments, employing some thirty-two persons. Gillespie had thirty-eight, employing some fifty-eight persons. These were divided as follows:

Comal County Industries.	Number of Establishments.	Number of Employees.
Brick kilns	2	4
Flour and meal	7	9
Sawed lumber	3	8
Liquors, malt	2	6
Sash, door and blinds	1	3
Soap and candles	1	2
Total:	16	32

It is noticeable that the Census does not mention the wagon factories for which New Braunfels, situated in Comal County, was noted.

---

[87] *Ibid*, p. 178.
[88] *Texas State Gazette*, Austin, December 25, 1858.

Gillespie County, Establishments.	Number of Establishments.	Number of Employees.
Liquors, malt	1	3
Lumber, sawed	2	4
Saddles and harness	3	5
Soaps and candles	1	1
Tin and sheet iron ware	2	3
Wagons, carts, etc.	6	9
Coopering	1	1
Flour and meal	4	8
Furniture cabinet	10	10
Blacksmithing	8	14
Total:	38	58

By the *Texas Almanac* for 1861, New Braunfels had a flour mill, four grist mills, two saw mills, one sash factory. All these were driven by water power. There were in Comal County two flour mills, nine grist mills, six saw mills, several shingle machines and two cotton gins.[89] In 1863 the Comal Cotton Manufacturing Company was chartered. It began manufacturing in 1865. From 1865-1867 there were manufactured 160,000 yards of domestics, 35,000 Osnaburgs, and 35,000 pounds of yarn. The labor was white, with the exception of three or four negro children. New Braunfels is said to be the first manufacturing town in the state. It contains a number of grist, flour and saw mills, several cotton gins and tanneries, several saddle tree factories and one sash and blind factory.[90] In 1868 a woolen factory was established at New Braunfels with a capital of $40,000. This was the New Braunfels Woolen Manufacturing Company. It turned out forty pairs of blankets and two hundred yards of tweeds or yarns a day. Raw material was furnished from the neighborhood and labor from the town.[91] There were, at that time, 30 dry goods stores, three flour mills, three saw mills, a large factory for woolen cloth, one for cotton cloth, a sash

---

[89] *Texas Almanac*, 1861, pp. 190-191.
[90] *Ibid*, 1868, pp. 180-181.
[91] *Ibid*, 1869, p. 150.

factory, and mechanic shops of every kind.[92] In 1870 Comal County had 84 establishments employing 202 hands. There were two steam engines and seven water wheels in the town. Austin County at that time had 105 establishments, employing 213 hands; Galveston County, 91 establishments, employing 533 hands. These counties had a far larger population to draw from than those in which the German element predominated. These were the only two counties in the State that in any way approached Comal County in manufacturing. The latter county supplied almost entirely the country in the neighborhood with wagons and carriages from its shops. It made from four to six thousand saddle trees annually.[93]

During Olmsted's stay in Texas he met a German scientist who had obtained seeds from Egypt, Algiers, Arabia and St. Helena. These he had planted and was trying to ascertain which were best adapted to the climate. Wheat growing of any kind at that time (1857) was a novelty. The Germans were not satisfied with corn and would not transport wheat from the North like the Anglo-American planters. They grew a great quantity of wheat and that with considerable success.[94] Silk culture has been tried among the Germans in Texas. One German in Brenham, Washington County, planted many hundred Japan and Italian mulberry trees. His experience taught him to believe that silk could be raised profitably in the Southern States.[95]

THE CULTURE OF COTTON AMONG THE GERMANS IN TEXAS.

The custom of the Germans of carrying on agriculture intensively is shown especially in the culture of cotton. In some cases their cotton fields were not more than an acre in extent.[96] As in Germany, so here, they used intelligent economy in their methods of cultivation.[97] Their fields looked as if they had been judiciously cultivated, and yielded a fine crop.[98] Their fields

[92] *Ibid.*
[93] *Guide to Western Texas*, 1876, p. 60.
[94] Olmsted, p. 170.
[95] *Jahrbuch für Texas*, 1882-84, p. 110.
[96] Olmsted, *Texas Journeys*, p. 141.
[97] *Ibid.* Also Von Halle, *Baumwoll Production*, p. 355.
[98] Olmsted, *supra*.

differed from those of the large planters in that the cotton had been picked with care and exactness.[99] None of the cotton had been permitted to go to waste. Their cotton, although the stalks were smaller than those of the planters, were much more even or regular in its growth,[100] Von Halle says, that the cotton raised by these Germans was known as "free cotton" in the North, and was sought after with great avidity by cotton manufacturers.[101] On account of its greater cleanliness, it brought in the market from one to two cents a pound more than that picked by slave labor in the same township.[102]

Of the foreign-born population in 1850, 1,866,397 were in the non-slave-holding states and 378,205 were in the slave-holding states. Few foreigners engaged in cotton culture, but where they did, they proved the fallacy of the statement that cotton could not be raised profitably with free labor.[103] The Germans in Texas produced more cotton to the acre and of better quality than that raised by slaves.[104] The comparison between slave labor and free labor was fair to the former. The soil was new, and slave labor was employed there with its maximum advantage.[105] The small farmer was at a disadvantage with the plantation owner, in that he had to pay a proportionally larger amount for fencing. The plantation owner had his own horses and mules. The small farmer, in many cases, could not afford to own the animals he used. The plantation owner in many cases had his own gin and press in the midst of his cotton fields. The small farmer had to send his cotton some distance to be cleaned, and often was at the mercy of the plantation owner. The planter could keep better informed on the fluctation of the market.[106] In one season it is said that the Germans of Texas would send 10,000 bales of cotton to the

---

[99] *Ibid.*
[100] *Ibid.*
[101] Von Halle, p. 201.
[102] Olmsted, *Cotton Kingdom,* II, p. 263. *Cf.* Speech by Cassius M. Clay, October 25, 1856; *Helper's Impending Crisis,* p. 207. Clay says he bases his statement on that of a slave owner.
[103] *Cf.* Hammond, M. B., *Cotton Industry,* p. 63.
[104] *Helper's Impending Crisis,* p. 207.
[105] Hammond, pp. 98-99.
[106] Olmsted, *Cotton Kingdom,* II, pp. 266-267.

market.¹⁰⁷ This was a large amount proportionally to the number of people. It is even stated that in 1858 half of the cotton grown in Texas is grown by white labor.¹⁰⁸ The *London News* of May 2, 1858, declares that:

"the proposals of slave trade, in the face of the success of the Germans in cotton cultivation, simply indicate the failure of slave labor in that State (Texas). * * * An arid desert lies behind the belt of German cultivation, and the slaveholders must contend with white labor or go back whence they came."¹⁰⁹

WAGES.

In 1847 the average daily wages was fifty cents with board. Men servants received from $10 to $20 a month; women servants from $5 to $12 a month.¹¹⁰ In the early fifties, in Texas, field workers received $7 to $10 a month and board; maid servants, $4 to $6 a month; cooks, $5 to $9; shepherds, $7 to $12 a month; tanners, $1.50 to $2 a day; masons, $1,50 to $2 per day; joiners, $1,50 to $2 a day; wagon makers, $10 a week; carpenters, $1,50 a day. When Olmsted was in Texas, the German farm laborers worked for $150 a year and clothed and insured themselves. This brought them in competition with slave labor. Slaves at that time brought $1,000. The German with that sum could hire six hands.¹¹¹ Journeymen were paid $15 a month and upwards and found. Farm laborers, $8 to $15 a month and board. Women servants $5 to $8.¹¹² The Comal Cotton Manufacturing Company paid in 1868 fifty cents a day for experienced spinners, and $2 a day for foremen.¹¹³ In the New Braunfels woolen mill, in 1868, wages varied from forty cents to $1.50 per day.¹¹⁴

Some of the German mechanics in the vicinity of New Braunfels made more money in one day, by going into the fields of the planters and picking side by side with the slaves, being paid by

---

[107] *Ibid.*
[108] *Southern Intelligencer*, Austin, December 22, 1858.
[109] Quoted, *Texas State Gazette*, Austin, May 15, 1858.
[110] Bracht, p. 98.
[111] Olmsted, p. 433.
[112] *Ibid*, p. 180.
[113] *Texas Almanac*, 1868, pp. 180-181.
[114] *Ibid*,

measure, than they could at their regular work in a week.[115] One woman in the first year she had ever seen a cotton field, picked more cotton in a day than any slave in the country.[116]

CHARACTER AND METHOD OF LIFE. GERMANS AND AMERICANS COMPARED.

There is perhaps no district of the United States where the Germans have kept their racial characteristics to so great a degree as in the district lying west of the Colorado river. The counties in which the "Adelsverein" founded its first communities are as German to-day in method of life, in sentiment and in culture, as they were when they were first founded. "Fifty-seven years of American residence has left a very distinct foreign flavor." [117] There you will see the German drinking his beer in small gardens. There you will hear music as it is sung in the Fatherland. There you will hear the German as the common speech. You might imagine yourself in one of the little towns of Germany.

The relation between the German and the American population during the time previous to the Civil War is an interesting topic. To-day, of course, relations are friendly, and in the cities such as Galveston and Houston, the German has become merged with the American population. This has not always been so. The comparison of the mode of life of the German with the American does not always favor the latter. It must be remembered that among the German population, brought over by the "Adelsverein", many were cultured men. Their leaders were educated men. Schools were early established. German and English were both taught.[118]

The attitude of the Germans toward slavery and the competition between free and slave labor necessarily brought the two elements of the population into conflict. The fact that German cotton brought a higher price in the market would naturally cause the American to look askance at the foreigner. Probably in no part of our Southern States was slave and free labor brought into

---

[115] Olmsted, *Cotton Kingdom*, II, p. 263.
[116] *Ibid.*
[117] *The Passing Show*, San Antonio, Texas, February 23, 1907.
[118] As early as August 1845 a school was established at New Braunfels

so great a contrast as in Texas. The population of the State was small. The State itself was new, and the German element was strong. In very few of our Southern States were there so many non-slave owners, and few had so many small proprietors. That many of the Germans were cultivated, is proved by the statements of both German and American writers. We shall leave the details of the attitude of the Germans toward slavery and their influence on the culture of the State to future chapters.

Bracht, writing in 1848, states that the Germans in Texas hold as firmly to the customs and speech of the Fatherland as they do in Pennsylvania.[119] Roemer in 1849 gives a good description of New Braunfels. All streets crossed each other at right angles and met in a public square.[120] The city was laid out after a regular plan. The houses were built after different plans; some were log houses, some built of limestone, and some were frame houses.[121] Many of the young men of the town ate at a restaurant kept by a former cook of a South-German nobleman. At her table gathered some ten or twelve young men. Many of them were former lieutenants in the armies of the German princes; some were former German students, merchants and farmers. The cooking was partly after the German and partly after the American custom.[122] On Sunday, dancing was commonly indulged in in accordance with the custom of the German peasants.[123]

Kapp, who visited the German settlements in 1852, describes New Braunfels as a well regulated place of about 2,000 inhabitants with some 200 houses. The main streets met in a square— the market place. All the streets were wide and were covered with beautiful trees, behind which simple, but well situated houses stood in gardens.

"I thought I was for a moment in one of those South-German villages where the children play on the streets with only their smocks on; where the mothers, working in the shade of their dwellings, while away a part of the day; and where little life is seen, because the men have something to do either in the fields or in their homes.

---

[119] Bracht, p. 107.
[120] Roemer, p. 117ff.
[121] Ibid, p. 118.
[122] Ibid, p. 124.
[123] Ibid, p. 121.

Everywhere I met German faces, German names, as well as German speech and customs; in the whole place there dwelled only a Scotchman and one American."[124]

He met a number of former German officials, officers, students and adventurers, who seemed to find themselves occupied as farmers, business men, guides or surveyors. Their faces as well as their hands showed the deep furrows of hard toil.[125] Olmsted gives the following description of New Braunfels:

"The main street of the town, * * * was very wide—three times as wide, in effect, as Broadway in New York. The houses, with which it was thickly lined on each side for a mile, were small, low cottages of no pretensions, yet generally looking neat and comfortable. Many were furnished with verandas and gardens, and the greater part were either stuccoed or painted. There were many workshops of small mechanics and small stores; * * * and bare-headed women, and men in caps and short jackets, with pendent pipes, were seen everywhere at work."[126]

The *Southern Intelligencer* states that the streets are broad and well laid out, and the banks are lined with ornamental and shade trees. No swine are allowed to run at large.[127]

From the very beginning the German element became conspicuous for its industry. The *Civilian and Galveston Gazette*, in an article regarding the Germans who came to Texas during the thirties, states that many brought nothing with them; that all had become independent. Many had become worth from $3,000 to $5,000.

"They now raise every year twice as much as they consume— have fine herds of cattle, horses and hogs; are out of debt; have a most scrupulous regard to punctuality in their contracts, and give indications of fine prosperity."[128]

The *Southern Intelligencer* under date of June 3, 1857, in describing the City of New Braunfels, declares that the town population, which consists mainly of Germans, is perhaps the most quiet, peaceable and industrious community to be found in this

---

[124] Kapp, *Aus und über Amerika*, Pt. II, p. 283ff.
[125] *Ibid.*
[126] *Texas Journeys*, pp. 142-143.
[127] *Southern Intelligencer*, Austin, June 3, 1857.

or in any other state.[129] In describing the Germans, Olmsted says they were to be seen, men, women and children, busy at some work.[130] He reports that in a conversation with an American farmer he learned that the Germans were not bad neighbors, but extremely useful and valuable ones; that their mechanics worked cheaply, steadily and excellently; that they had been very honest and trustworthy in their dealings; that they were every year improving about their houses and building new houses which were more comfortable than their old ones; that they worked their little pieces of land "first-rate".[131] The *Texas State Gazette* declares that wherever they have settled in any considerable number the country around them looks more thriving and flourishing than in most other portions.[132] The following taken from the same journal under date of September 6, 1858, shows the condition of the settlements founded by Castro:

"Twelve years ago Castroville was one of the most attractive hunting grounds of the fierce Lipan Indians. It derives its name from Mr. Castro, who obtained in or about 1842, a colonization contract from the Texan government, and is still living in the town with his family.

"The majority of the settlers are from the French and German borders of the Rhine, and seem to be hardy and hard-working fellows. They speak German among themselves. * * *

"The town numbers 1000 inhabitants within the incorporated limits, independent of a large population in the close neighborhood. Three other settlements, Quihi, Vandenburgh and Dhanis are settled west of Castroville, and are improving fast."[133]

It is said that the majority of the hand workers and retailers of Galveston in 1845 were Germans.[134] Siemering states that in the early eighties one-half of the property was in the hands of that race.[135] Olmsted says:

"The poor immigrants who were able to purchase farms have made the happiest progress, meeting a steady market for their production, and a continuous appreciation in the value of their im-

---
[129] *Ibid*, note 1, *supra*.
[130] *Texas Journeys*, p. 140.
[131] *Ibid*, p. 139.
[132] *State Gazette*, Austin, June 30, 1855.
[133] *Ibid*, September 6, 1856
[134] Roemer, p. 59.

proved lands. The mechanics and laborers, after the first distress, found more work awaiting them than their hands could perform, and have constantly advanced to become employers, offering their old wages to the newcomers of each successive emigration."[136]

The following is quoted from Olmsted, because it describes the character of this people so well:

"The first German settlers we saw, we knew at once. They lived in little log cabins and had inclosures of ten acres of land about them. The cabins were very simple and cheap habitations, but there were very many little conveniences about them and a care to secure comfort in small ways that was very agreeable to notice.[137] * * *

"I never in my life, except, perhaps, in awakening from a dream, met with such a sudden and complete transfer of associations. Instead of loose boarded or hewn log walls, with crevices stuffed with rags or daubed with mortar, which we had been accustomed to see during the last month, on staving in a door where we have found any to open; instead, even, of four bare, cheerless sides of whitewashed plaster, which we have found twice or thrice in a more aristocratic American residence, we were—in short, we were in Germany.

"There was nothing wanting for one of those delightful little inns which the pedestrian who has tramped through the Rhineland will ever remember gratefully. A long room, extending across the whole front of the cottage, the walls pink, with stenciled panels and scroll ornaments in crimson, and with neatly framed and glazed pretty lithographic prints hanging on all sides; a long, thick, dark oak table with rounded ends, oak benches at its sides; chiseled oak chairs; a sofa, covered with cheap pink calico, with a small vine pattern, a stove in the corner, a little mahogany cupboard in another corner, with picture and glasses upon it; a smoky atmosphere; and, finally, four thick-bearded men from whom the smoke proceeds, who all bow and say 'Good morning', as we lift our hats in the doorway.

"The landlady enters; she does not readily understand us, and one of the smokers rises immediately to assist us. Dinner we shall have immediately, and she spreads the white cloth at an end of the table before she leaves the room, and in two minutes' time * * *, we are asked to sit down. An excellent soup is set before us, and in succession there follow two courses of meat, neither of them pork and neither of them fried, two dishes of vegetables, salad, compoté of peaches, coffee with milk, wheat bread from the loaf, and beautiful and sweet butter—not only such butter as I have never tasted south of the Potomac before, but such as I have been told a thousand times it was impossible to make in the southern

---

[136] *Texas Journeys*, p. 430ff.
[137] *Ibid*, p. 140.

climate. What is the secret? I suppose it is extreme cleanliness, beginning far back of where cleanliness usually begins in the South, and careful and thorough working.

"We then spent an hour in conversation with the gentlemen who were in the room. They were all educated, cultivated well-bred, respectful, kind and affable men. All were natives of Germany and had been living several years in Texas. Some of them were travelers, their homes being in other German settlements; some of them had resided long at Braunfels.

"It was so very agreeable to meet such men again, and the account they gave of the Germans in Texas was so interesting and so gratifying that we were unwilling to immediately continue our journey. We went out to look at our horses; a man in cap and jacket was rubbing their legs—the first time they had received such attention in Texas, except from ourselves, or by special and costly arrangement with a negro. They were pushing their noses into racks filled with fine mesquit hay—the first they had had in Texas. They seemed to look at us imploringly. We ought to spend the night. But there is evidently no sleeping room for us in the little inn. They must be full. But then we could sleep with more comfort on the floor here, probably, than we had been accustomed to of late. We concluded to ask if they could accommodate us for the night. Yes, with pleasure—would we be pleased to look at the room they could afford us? Doubtless in the cock-loft. No, it was another little cottage in the rear. A little room had been provided, with blue walls again, and oak furniture; two beds, one of them would be for each of us—the first time we had been offered the luxury of sleeping alone in Texas; two large windows with curtains, and evergreen roses trained over them on the outside—not a pane of glass missing or broken—the first sleeping room we have had in Texas where this was the case; a bureau, on which were a complete set of the Conversations Lexicon; Kendall's Santa Fé Expedition; a statuette in porcelain; plants in pots; a brass study lamp; a large ewer and basin for washing, and a couple of towels of thick stuff, full a yard and a quarter long. O, yes, it will do admirably; we will spend the night. * * *

"As I was returning to the inn about ten o'clock, I stopped for a few minutes at the gate of one of the little cottages to listen to some of the best singing I have heard for a long time, several parts being sustained by very sweet and well-trained voices. * * *

"In the morning we found that our horses had been bedded for the first time in Texas.

"As we rode out of town it was delightful to meet again troops of children, with satchels and knapsacks of books and little kettles of dinner, all with ruddy, cheerful faces, the girls especially so, with hair braided neatly and without caps or bonnets, smiling and saluting us—'guten morgen'—as we met. Nothing was so pleasant in Texas before; hardly in the South."[188]

---

[188] *Texas Journeys*, p. 143ff.

The same writer met several educated Germans during his travels in Western Texas. Here is his description of one of them:

"There is something extremely striking in the incongruities and bizarre contrasts of the backwoods life of these settlers. You are welcomed by a figure in blue flannel shirt and pendant beard, quoting Tacitus, having in one hand a long pipe, in the other a butcher's knife; Madonnas upon log walls; coffee in tin cups upon Dresden saucers; barrels for seats, to hear a Beethoven symphony on the grand piano; 'My wife made these pantaloons and my stockings grew in the field yonder.' A fowling-piece that cost $300 and a saddle that cost $5; a bookcase half filled with classics, half with sweet potatoes."[139] These educated men were "still able to sustain their intellectual life and retain their refined taste; and, more than all, with their antecedents to be seemingly content and happy, while under the necessity of supporting life in the most frugal manner by hard labor."[140]

At Sisterdale he met several cultivated men. This was the so-called Latin settlement of which an uncle of Kapp's was a member. "The gentlemen we met were two of these singular settlers; one of them, the schoolmaster, a Berlin student, the other a baron, over whose Texan 'domain' we were actually passing. He took us to his castle, which was near by. It was a new log house. The family occupied a lean-to in the rear, as the roof was not quite finished. * * *

"A few minutes brought us to the judge's house, a double log cabin upon a romantic rocky bluff of the Guadaloupe. He came out to receive us * * * . He was partly bald, but seemed to have an imperturbable and happy good-nature that gave him eternal youth. A genial cultivation beamed from his face. He had been a man of marked attainments at home (an intimate associate with Humboldt and a friend of Goethe's Bettina), and kept up here a warm love for nature. His house was the very picture of good-nature, science and backwoods. Romances and philosophies were piled in heaps in a corner of the logs. A dozen guns and rifles and a Madonna in oil, after Murillo, filled a blank on the wall. Deer-skins covered the bed, clothes hung about upon antlers, snake-skins were stretched to dry upon the bedstead, barometer, whisky, powder-horn, and specimens of Saxony wool occupied the table.

"The dinner was Texan, of corn-bread and frijoles, with coffee served in tin cups, but the salt was Attic and the talk was worthy of golden goblets."[141]

Let us contrast with these descriptions those which the same

---

[139] *Ibid*, p. 430.

[140] *Ibid*, pp. 429-430.

[141] *Ibid*, p. 191-193. This last passage has reference to Ottomar von Behr, whose work we have referred to often.

author gives regarding the Anglo-American population of the State. He says that in his whole route through Eastern Texas he did not see one of the inhabitants look into a newspaper or a book, although he had spent days in houses where men were lounging about the fire without occupation.[142] Contrast the following description which he gives of a hotel in Austin, with the inn at New Braunfels. He says:

"We had reckoned upon getting some change of diet when we reached the capital of the State, and upon having good materials not utterly spoiled by carelessness, ignorance, or nastiness in cooking. We had reckoned without our host.

"We arrived in a norther and were shown, at the hotel to which we had been recommended, into an exceedingly dirty room in which two of us slept with another gentleman, who informed us that it was the best room in the house. The outside door opening upon the ground, had no latch, and during the night it was blown open by the norther, and, after we had made two ineffectual attempts to barricade it, was kept open until morning. Before daylight a boy came in and threw down an armful of wood by the fireplace. He appeared half an hour or two afterwards and made a fire. When the breakfast bell rung we all turned out in haste, though our boots were gone and there was no water. At this moment, as we were reluctantly pulling on our clothing, a negro woman burst into the room, leaving the door open, and laid a towel on the wash-table. * * *

"When finally we got to breakfast and had offered us—but I will not mention the three articles—only the 'fry' had been changed for the worse before it was fried—we naturally began to talk of changing our quarters and trying another of the hotels. Then up spoke a dark, sad man at our side: 'You can't do better than stay here; I have tried both the others, and I came here yesterday because the one I was at was *too dirty!*' * * * Never did we see any wholesome food on that table. It was a succession of burnt meat of swine and of bulls, decaying vegetables and sour and moldy farinaceous glues, all pervaded with rancid butter."[143]

The other inns at which he stopped on his journey through Eastern Texas were even worse than this.[144] He states that he met with wheat bread only twice out of the city of Austin. His experiences in the homes of the settlers were more disagreeable than those he met with in the inns.

---
[142] *Ibid*, p. 111.
[143] *Ibid*, pp. 60 and 103.
[144] Olmsted, *Cotton Kingdom*, Vol. II, p. 10.

The windows of the houses were usually without panes. The rooms were open to the rafters, and the doors closed with difficulty. The usual meal consisted of pork, salt and fresh, cold cornbread and boiled sweet potatoes. "There is always, too, the black decoction of the South called coffee, than which it is often difficult to imagine any beverage more revolting". He describes a house of a man who had emigrated to Texas from the North twenty years before as being more comfortless than nine-tenths of the stables at the North.[145] There was not a pane of glass in the house. Some of the windows were boarded over, some had wooden shutters and some were entirely open.

He states that he met several cultivated and educated men in Austin, and says that none of the legislative bodies he had seen commanded his respect for the simple, manly dignity of their members, and the trustworthiness for the duties that engaged them, more that the General Assembly of Texas. "There was honest eloquence displayed at every opportunity for its use, and business was carried on with great rapidity, but with complete parliamentary regularity, and all desirable gentlemanly decorum." [146]

RELATIONS BETWEEN GERMANS AND AMERICANS.

From the time that the Germans settled in great numbers in Texas, there were disagreements between them and the Anglo-American population. This was due to a great extent to slavery, and to the fact that the Germans did not mingle much with the American population. The fact that the Germans were settled together and at some distance from the Americans, tended to separate the two races. Solms-Braunfels' work may have had some influence in bring this about. Roemer states that the book's weak side lies in the prejudicial and unjust judgments regarding the Anglo-American population of Texas. Single mistakes become the vices of the whole population.[147] The *Houston Telegraph* states that Solms' book is hindering emigration to the United States.[148]

---

[145] *Ibid, Cotton Kingdom*, pp. 14-15.
[146] *Texas Journeys*, pp. 112-114.
[147] Roemer, p. 44.
[148] *Houston Telegraph*, March 30, 1848.

Solms declares that the Americans of Texas do not belong to the better class of their nation. The chief characteristic of the American is greed for gold. To this "Mammon" he sacrifices all: it is the basis of his whole existence. The home of his parents, souvenirs of friends, things, which to the German have value, are prostituted by the American, if he can cover them with money. The more business of this kind, the greater will be his reputation as a "smart man". If the immigrant has business with the Americans, he can be certain of his losing his last shirt. The American will seek to ensnare him by means of pretensions and promises. If the good natured, trusting German gives way to him, he will treat him more severely than a slave. The people who came to Texas in the earlier days were almost all criminals who had to flee from the United States. It is well known that the first offices and places of the Republic were in the hands of people of this character. In a word, the foreigner can be assured that the American advances against him by means of fraud, and will find his advantage in some way, of which the European has no presentiment. The American is bold and enterprising in carrying out his plans and speculation. No privation, no fatigue, no danger, will keep him from doing so. The prince says that a wild country such as Texas is naturally the abode of adventurers. He styles these "Loofers".[149] This work must have had an influence in maintaining in the German an idea that the Americans were a people to be avoided.

From an early period, slavery had an influence in causing a lack of harmony between these two different elements in the population. As early as 1849, the planters were jealous of European immigrants. It was felt that a struggle over the relations between the German and Anglo-American was imminent.[150] The Germans were naturally abolitionists and felt that slavery lessened their own value.[151] A large proportion of the immigrants remained apart in German communities.[152] Those in the

---

[149] Solms Braunfels, Texas, *Ein Handbuch für Auswanderer nach Texas.* Frankfurt, a M., 1846, p. 36ff.

[150] Smith, Edward, M. D., *Account of a Journey through Northeastern Texas in 1849,* p. 89.

[151] *Ibid.*

[152] Olmsted, *Texas Journeys,* p. 431.

cities had little influence. In social and political relations the Germans did not occupy the position which their numbers entitled them to. In the period before the Civil War, they mingled little with the Americans, except for the necessary buying and selling. The Americans had the prestige of pre-occupation. Their rule over slaves and Mexicans made them more or less domineering in their attitude toward the new comers.[153] The manners and the ideals of the Texans and of the Germans were hopelessly divergent.[154] "They made little acquaintance, observing one another, partly with unfeigned curiosity, often tempered with mutual contempt."[155] A conversation reported by Olmsted gives an idea of the sentiment held by the American toward the German. The speaker said "the Dutch" he had seen in the North were very different from those in this country. There, they were industrious and minded their own business. Here, they did not appear to have any business. The master of the house, in which the conversation occurred, said that he refused them fire and water as outlaws whenever he had an opportunity.[156]

The *Southern Intelligencer* gives the following ironical comment on the pardoning of a Captain Barton, who flogged a discharged German soldier, named Head:

"Our friends should recollect that Barton was an army officer of Virginia and Head was only a poor devil of a 'German who had to work for his living,' and was therefore 'degraded to the level of the negro.' If so degraded, why not whip him? Is there not danger that he and his countrymen might make cotton at ten cents per pound and thereby defeat the notion of the Gonzales aristocrats who believed that the making of cotton by 'poor white folks' should be headed off."[157]

In reporting that several hundred Germans had arrived, the *State Gazette* hopes they will scatter.

"It is from a want of due regard to the circumstances that we witness so marked a want of sympathy between the German and American population."[158]

---

[153] *Texas Journeys*, p. 431.
[154] *Ibid.*
[155] *Ibid.*
[156] *Ibid*, p. 132.
[157] *Southern Intelligencer*, Austin, June 8, 1859.
[158] *Texas State Gazette*, Austin, June 16, 1855.

A speech delivered in 1853, quoted by Busey in his work on Immigration, a work written in behalf of "Know-Nothingism", shows that the Germans had an antipathy to the rule of the Americans. The speech was given at New Braunfels by a Mr. Wipprecht, and in concluding his speech, he is quoted as having said:

"Now, let us manfully and firmly oppose the arrogant assumption and overbearing of these natives. Let us oppose their further extension of this slave-holding population in Western Texas, for we have cultivated and settled this country before the natives thought of doing so."[159]

In May, 1854, a convention of Germans was held at San Antonio, Texas. They drew up resolutions, some of which demanded that criminal and civil laws be enacted, so simple and intelligible that there should be no need of lawyers; the abolition of the grand jury; the abolition of capital punishment; the abolition of all temperance laws; that a man be taxed in accordance with his income, the greater the income, the greater the tax; that there should be no religious instruction in the schools and no teacher who is a preacher; the abolition of laws respecting Sunday or days of prayer; the abolition of the oath as a matter of religious sanction; that Congress should never be opened by prayer.[160] In commenting upon this platform, the "Texas Gazette" says:

"The German population in Texas, in the language of one of their number who is an honor to his native land, has been treated liberally and with more true benevolence than in any other State in the Union, and if in return, they are engaged in forming secret societies, in league with similar societies among the fanatics of the North, to undermine and uproot our institutions and laws, religion and its ministers, it is time the people of the State should know it."[161]

This platform brought letters to the various newspapers of the State. Editorials were written regarding it. The following letter, date New Braunfels, June 20, 1855, will show the feeling aroused among both classes of the population. The letter was

---

[159] Busey, *Immigration*, p. 32. It is quoted from the *New Orleans Creole*.
[160] *Texas State Gazette*, June 22, 1854.
[161] *Ibid.*

in reply to one of June 16, of that year, signed "Curtius". The letter reads as follows:

"In the Texas *State Times* of the 16th. inst., there appeared an article signed 'Curtius,' which charges the German population of Western Texas with having assumed toward the native-born citizens and their institutions, domestic and political, an attitude which is becoming of serious moment in this part of the State * * *

"Mr. 'Curtius' asks 'who are the Germans of Texas then and what are they doing?' and says, 'They Are The Escaped Victims of Foreign Tyranny And Despotism.' Now, I would answer this question in a different way. The Germans are industrious, peaceable, law-abiding citizens, who have contributed very much wherever they have settled in the United States to the prosperity of the country, a fact fully acknowledged by the American public journals. * * * What was the Guadaloupe valley and the country west of it, before these Germans arrived? What is it now? Who contributed more to the prosperity of that part of Texas than those Germans? In 1844, when your correspondent arrived here, Lavaca, Victoria, Gonzales and Seguin, were very small places, containing but few inhabitants, with little or no trade, and money exceedingly scarce. Beyond Seguin, there was no sign of civilization, San Antonio excepted. * * * Who went forward to the frontier without even the least protection from the government? Forsooth, the Germans. It is well known that when, in 1846, the German emigration company wanted to settle their emigrants on the Perdinales, about seventy miles from all settlements, in the middle of the Indian Territory, the Governor of Texas said that he would not give them any protection; but, in spite of that, those Germans advanced thither, when the freight to New Braunfels was from $3 to $4 per 100 pounds, on account of the Mexican War, and besides there was much sickness then prevailing in Western Texas. Notwithstanding these and many other contending difficulties, the German colonists went up there * * * and protected themselves under countless privations; * * * . Still, through their perseverance and energy, they improved the lands, founded the town of Fredericksburg, * * *. These Germans in 1847-1848 went thirty-six miles further to the Llano, and thereby actually reached Fisher and Miller's grant, and they have there still some very fine settlements. * * *

"Mr. 'Curtius' charges the Germans with treason on account of their 'famous platform convention and their annual singing societies, as they are termed, where they are called together from every part of the State annually, and there hidden from the eyes of the native citizens, they resolve to abolish the Presidency, the Sabbath, grand juries, etc., and conspire to do other things, which are never known except by accident and are abominable to native Americans.'"

"The writer answers this by stating that the singing societies of the different settlements meet for the purpose of singing and amusement. The Americans were not invited, because they had no societies. The writer claims further that the platform was formed by a few Germans, not natives of the United States, who did not understand what they were doing.

The Germans of New Braunfels were accused of mobbing a lawyer and ordering all the Americans to leave that place before a specified time. This was denied by the writer quoted above.[162]

The *Indianola Bulletin* declares that the Germans as a whole were not the originators of the animosity existing between them and the native citizens; that whatever trouble has arisen between the two elements of the population, has been caused by a few fanatics among them.[163]

A convention of the citizens of Comal County was held at New Braunfels June 26, 1855, and resolutions were adopted. In the resolutions it was declared, that the Germans did not have any hostile feelings toward the Americans; that they acknowledged their allegiance to the laws of Texas and the United States.[164]

Busey states that the *Galveston Zeitung* of August 19, 1855, the organ of the Germans in Texas, contained the following statement:

"You have often observed that the continual clashing between natives and foreigners might easily come to a general eruption, which would result disastrously to the Germans, unless we consider in time the proverb that, 'He who desires peace should prepare for war.'

"The Cincinnati April Scenes and those at Columbus, have shown that the police in such cases are not fully sufficient for our guard, or suppression of the mob. In such cases, we must depend upon ourselves to defend our families and property, as is our duty and right. Without an organization, this is impossible. In the moment of an attack, it is too late to form such an organization; our duty is to organize beforehand. I therefore submit the following proposition:

"'1st. To form in every town, where there is sufficient German population, one or more guard companies who shall furnish their arms.

"'2nd. The uniform must be everywhere the same, to preserve equality. The uniform is necessary to prevent confusion and to distinguish our friends.

---
[162] *Texas State Gazette*, June 30, 1855.
[163] *Indianola Bulletin*, quoted in *Texas State Gazette*, June 30, 1855.
[164] *Texas State Gazette*, July 11, 1855.

"'3d. The arms must be everywhere the same and we recommend as the best arms (those) of the Turners and revolvers.

"'4th. A member of any company shall be recognized as a member wherever there be such a company formed. All the companies in the United States must be in connection with one chief or leader.

"'5th. The decade system is the most commendable; *i. e.*, every ten members to constitute one decade and make one leader, who in case of necessity can call together his nine comrades. The leaders then elect their officers. Five decades would be enough for one company.'"[165]

All sorts of rumors were prevalent regarding the German population. "Know-Nothingism" was at its height. Slavery was thought to be threatened. The Germans of New Braunfels, in a letter dated August 18, 1855, called upon the Chief Justice of Comal County, W. A. Andross, to reply to newspaper accounts which stated that the Germans were hostile to the Americans. Andross said that he found the Germans friendly and courteous to the Americans; that the charges made against them, that they had ordered the Americans to leave the town, were untrue; that many of the officers of the County, which was predominantly German, were Americans.[166]

It was rumored that an officer in the Texan "Rangers" had had a pitched battle with the Germans, and some twenty Germans had been killed and more wounded. This was declared to be false.[167]

The *State Gazette,* in an article entitled "Know-Nothingism in Texas", declares that the American party was preventing immigration; that 200 immigrants had arrived at Indianola October 2, 1855, and that only 80 remained on account of persecutions waged against foreigners. It further states that a project was on foot among the Germans of several places in Texas to emigrate to Costa Rica.[168]

An article in the same journal shows the attitude of the Germans toward politics. The battle cry of the democracy, "Equal rights for all and special privileges for none", appealed

---

[165] Busey, *Immigration*, p. 28.
[166] *Texas State Gazette*, September 16, 1855.
[167] *Ibid*, October 6, 1855.
[168] *Ibid*, October 20, 1855.

to them. The growing power of the Know-Nothing party in Texas caused them to swell the democratic ranks. The article in question is headed, "Who controls the German vote?" and says:

"The German vote is controlled by no one, nor by any party; they cannot be 'teased,' 'whipped in' or 'marshalled' by any one. Whoever thinks that the Germans as a mass are not able to control themselves; that they need advice; that they may be used as tools or footballs; or that they may be turned one way or the other: he is most certainly mistaken. * * *
"We Germans, as a mass, are Democrats. * * * The generality of the German population of the State of Texas are true, whole, uncontrolled and sound Democrats."[169]

It was claimed that the Germans, during an election in the fifties, held at one of the interior towns of Texas, marched in a body to the polls. They paraded their own flag, and marched through the streets singing German national airs.[170] This was probably simply a patriotic movement, which to-day would cause no comment. The Southerner thought that every meeting of these people was a move against his cherished "institution" of slavery. Their singing societies and their "Turnvereins" appeared to him as secret societies aimed at the destruction of American government and institutions. Some of the papers recognized the fact that the Germans were peaceable and law abiding. As time went on, the Germans and Americans more easily amalgamated. The German saw that it was for his interest to do nothing reflecting in any way on slavery. The *Southern Intelligencer* in 1859 stated that it preferred German immigration to that from the North.[171] It is doubtless true that the presence of the Germans would not have caused any comment had it not been for the rise of "Know-Nothingism." That movement tended to cause the Germans to vote as a unit, and to take part in politics. This aroused the ire of the Southerner and hence caused the races to grow apart.

[169] *Ibid*, July 11, 1857.
[170] Busey, p. 30.
[171] *Southern Intelligencer*, Austin, April 6, 1859.

CHAPTER V.

SLAVERY. NUMBER OF NEGROES IN THE GERMAN SETTLEMENTS. ATTITUDE OF GERMANS TOWARD SLAVERY, SECESSION AND RECONSTRUCTION.

The Germans by disposition and training were opposed to slavery. They considered it an evil and felt that it lessened the value of their own labor. Settling in communities as they did in Western Texas, slave and free labor did not come into conflict to any great extent. A writer in 1849 states that the introduction of Germans and other Europeans "is going on with great rapidity, that they were usually poor and had early imbibed an abolitionist spirit; that it was felt that a struggle was ready to commence, and that Texas would be greatly agitated over this question; that already the planters were jealous of European immigration.[1]

That the American Government took an interest in the introduction of the European immigrants into Texas, is shown by the correspondence of Secretary of State Upshur with Edward Everett, United States Minister to England, and with General W. S. Murphy, Chargé d'affaires of the United States in Texas.[2] To the latter he writes as follows:

"If Texas should not come into our Union, measures will be taken to fill her territory with emigrants from Europe. Extensive arrangements for this are already made, and they will be carried into effect as soon as the decision of Texas shall be known. These emigrants will bring with them European feelings and European opinions. Emigration from the United States will cease; at all events, the people of the Southern States will not run the hazard of subjecting their slave property to the control of a population who are anxious to abolish slavery. Texas will soon cease to be an American state. Her population, her politics and her manners, will stamp her as European. This fact alone will destroy the sympathy which now exists between that country and the United States.

"But the first measures of the new emigrants, as soon as they shall have sufficient strength, will be to destroy that great domestic

---

[1] Smith, *Journey through Northeastern Texas*, 1849.
[2] Cf. Correspondence, *Senate Documents*, 28th Congress, 1st Session, Doc. 341.

institution, upon which, so much of the prosperity of our Southern country depends. To this England will stimulate them, and she will also furnish the means of accomplishing it. * * * I will only add, that if Texas should not be attached to the United States, she cannot maintain that institution ten years." [3]

This letter suggests an interesting speculation. What might have been the result if Texas had not been annexed? The increasing number of immigrants and their settlement at one point might have made it no impossibility for slavery to have been kept from their borders, and part of the country, at least, might have become free territory.

There are several reasons why these propositions did not come true so far as Western Texas was concerned. The planters, on account of the great numbers of Germans, did not settle that territory. There was a competition of interests between the free and slave labor. The territory was very near the border, and made it convenient for runaway slaves to escape into Mexico;[4] it was also too near the territory of the Indians and slaves would be in danger of being taken as booty by them; it was also a long distance from a market, making the culture of cotton less profitable. The great pasture lands were more suited to grazing. Negroes were not adapted to looking after herds, where they would have to be isolated and at a distance from overseers. These facts kept the planters from the country occupied by the Germans and lessened the danger of a conflict over the question of slavery.[5]

"As to slavery, the mass existing among themselves, where no slaves are seen, and having no instinctive prejudice of color, feel simply the natural repugnance for a system of forced labor universal in free society. Few of them concern themselves with the theoretical right or wrong of the institution, and while it does not interfere with their own liberty or progress, are indifferent of its existence." [6]

---

[3] Letter of A. P. Upshur, Secretary of State, dated Washington, January 16, 1844. *Ibid*, p. 46.

[4] Kapp states that 150 negroes escaped into Mexico in 1854. *N. Y. Tribune*, January 20, 1855.

[5] For the above, cf. *Texas Journeys*, pp. 440-441.

[6] *Ibid*, p. 433.

The authors of handbooks and other works written to stimulate immigration, attempted to prove that slavery did not have a strong hold on Texas. The pamphlet, issued by the Adelsverein, announcing its plans, quotes a letter written to the Augsburg *Allegemeine Zeitung* by a German in Texas, who states that he is opposed to slavery; that the plantations in Texas are small and that slaves "are made one of the family;" he hopes that the influence of the North and of England will root out slavery. He says that the number of negroes in relation to the size of the land is small.[7] Martin, in his book which was written to induce Germans to settle in Texas, declares that no slavery is allowed in the territory of the German Colonization Society.[8] Beyer, writing in 1846, states that no slavery is permitted in the German colonies; that it is the established opinion that with the increase of the German population, slavery will entirely disappear from Texas.[9] He further states:

"It has been asserted that the cultivation of cotton, sugar and tobacco, in the hot climate is too difficult for whites, but the contrary has been proved by thousands of examples." [10]

These will suffice to show the attempts to discountenance the existence of slavery in Texas, and to influence the Germans to immigration, showing that the writers recognized that the known antipathy of the Germans to slavery should be overcome.

Many writers wrote regarding slavery in Texas, and these works probably added to the German's previous dislike to that institution. Solms-Braunfels, through his influence as Commissioner-General of the Adelsverein, must have been a factor in keeping away Germans from Texas on account of his descriptions of slavery in that State. Whether or not his book had any influence in hindering immigration, it must have had an influence in increasing whatever dislike they may have had for that institution. He says:

---
[7] Letter of *Augsburger Allgemeine Zeitung*, December 9, 1844; quoted in Texas, *Ein Handbuch für deutsche Auswanderer*. Bremen, 1846.
[8] Martin, *Die Deutsche Gesellschaft für Texas in Biebrich*. Wiesbaden, 1848, p. 13.
[9] Beyer, M., *Das Auswanderungsbuch, oder Führer und Rathgeber bei der Auswanderung nach Nord Amerika und Texas*. Leipzig, 1846, p. 149.
[10] Ibid.

"To me personally (and I hope the same is also so for the majority of my countrymen) it is not evident why these men to whom almighty God gave a black colored skin, should belong to others to whom He gave a white skin, to treat as a horse, a dog, * * * But the free-born Americans, whose land is the freeest in the world, whose laws and institutions are the best planned in the world, do not find it odious that these unfortunate negroes, after being mixed with the blood of whites until the fifth generation, should be cast under the yoke of a slavery, which would be degrading to an animal.

"The negroes found in Texas are certainly not from Africa, but they are brought from the United States, and it is the simplest and easiest thing to escape the English and French ships cruising about the African coast. There are in the United States complete negro breeding places from which those raised are brought to the slave market at New Orleans. Here are seen hundreds offered for sale, and the brokers, by whom they are offered for sale, praise their nefarious business. Buyers go to the sales, as they would to their work, or as we go to the inspection of the horses of a trader.

"It is now freely said, that the negroes are spared and well treated, since they represent an important capital. This ought to be the case if one holds the principle of slavery to be permissible. I have seen them in Louisiana plantations, where the negroes were well treated, and appeared to be well inclined toward their masters. Their welfare depends, however, on the whim or feelings of the master, and if they are well clothed and nourished, on the other hand, an angry master will cast upon them more blows than a mild, calm owner. More still, upon the whim or feeling of the master, depends the treatment of the slave by each of his overseers. These are always Americans and usually rough men. With their each momentary whim or predilection for this or that negress, the treatment of the poor blacks entrusted to them is decided. They have full right to lash, when it pleases them, also the right to shoot them down on the occasion of any revolt. What man of honor or feeling will allow himself to engage in this business which allows them to bind calmly to a tree these unfortunate creatures, who dare not refuse to submit, and to punish them with as many as a hundred lashes of the whip; or at night spying about their dwellings, to listen to their conversation in order to find out some plot of flight?"

The prince states that negroes are hunted with hounds; that he had seen a pack of hounds used for that purpose himself; that the Americans defend themselves on the ground that the negro is not the intellectual equal of the white. He says that every precaution is taken to prevent them from learning or advancing. He states that he found "more honesty, more fidelity, more attachment, more thankfulness among them, generally more sense, than among many Americans or European Americans."[11]

Roemer advises his countrymen not to emigrate to Texas on account of slavery. He prefers the Western and Northwestern States for that reason. He says:

"In all slaveholding states, the position of the free workman, dependent upon their own labor, who is not a slave owner, is much less agreeable than in the free states, and is always to the slave-owning planter, more or less subordinate. Wholly influenced by the somewhat decided inclination against negro slavery, very few German immigrants will find themselves in a position to purchase negroes. The great majority will be compelled to rely upon the labor of their own hands, and hence must be concerned by the disadvantages mentioned." [12]

From the earliest period of German colonization, few Germans were slave owners. Sommer mentions a German, in 1845, who possessed a negro and a negress.[13] Roemer states in 1846, that many German families were settled in the territory between the Brazos and Colorado, namely, in the neighborhood of Industry and Cummins Creek, and that only a few were plantation owners and possessors of slaves.[14] In 1856, when Olmsted visited New Braunfels, which then had a population of three thousand, there was an American planter in the neighborhood who owned one hundred negroes, an American in the town, owning one negro girl and a German who hired one as a domestic.[15] The same writer states that he did not meet one German slave owner among the Germans of Western Texas.[16] He states that a citizen of San Antonio, who, on account of business relations with the Germans was well informed in the matter, told him that he knew, in all, of twelve German slave proprietors in Texas. Ten of these had unwillingly bought housemaids to relieve their wives, who were unable to find German servants; one man owned four

---

[11] Solms-Braunfels, Carl Prinz zu, Texas, etc. Frankfurt a. M., 1846, p. 39ff.

[12] Roemer, p. 40.

[13] Sommer, 1846, pp. 74-75.

[14] Roemer, p. 20. This refers to the settlements of the thirties founded by Ernst, Kleberg, et al.

[15] Olmsted, *Texas Journeys*, pp. 180-181.

[16] *Ibid*, p. 432.

field hands in Gillespie County; another about the same number in Washington County—both old Texans of '36.[17]

According to the Census of 1850, Comal County contained sixty-one negroes out of a total population of 1723; Gillespie, in which Fredericksburg was situated, five negroes out of a population of 1176; Medina, in which Castroville was situated, twenty-eight negroes out of a population of 909.[18] According to the *Texas Almanac*, Comal County had in 1855, 126 negroes, and Gillespie County, 63;[19] and in 1856 Comal County had 163 and Gillespie County 100 negroes, respectively.[20] Olmsted gives the total population for 1857 of Comal County as 3500 and Gillespie 2000.[21] The Census of 1870 gives as the population for 1860, of Comal County as 4030 and Gillespie County 2736.[22] The *Texas Almanac* states that Comal County had 243 negroes and Gillespie County 30 negroes in 1860.[23] This shows that in these counties where the Verein settled its colonies, and where Germans were the predominating race, that the number of negroes was comparatively small. If we take in consideration the fact that many of these may have been free negroes and that those who were not may have been owned by Americans, it shows that very few Germans, if any, were possessors of slaves.[24]

There were two rival parties among the Germans.[25] The office holders and those who saw that it was for their interest and material advancement were friendly to the slave party. Many were, no doubt, adherents of the Democratic party because of principle. They believed that that was the party of the people. Its slogan "equal rights for all and special privileges for none," appealed to their democratic instincts.[26] There was no

---

[17] *Ibid*, footnote.
[18] *Census* 1850, p. 503.
[19] *Texas Almanac*, 1857, pp. 69-70.
[20] *Ibid*.
[21] Olmsted, *Texas Journeys*, p. 428, footnote.
[22] *Census*, 1870.
[23] *Texas Almanac*, 1861.
[24] In 1870 there were only about a dozen negroes in Gillespie County, which had a population at that time of 3500. *Texas Almanac*, 1871, p. 102.
[25] Cf. Olmsted, *Texas Journeys*, p. 434.
[26] Cf. *Supra*, Ch. IV, p. 211.

party to which an anti-slavery man could belong. There was little opportunity in a slave State for discussion of the question of slavery, so there was little chance to show great activity. The revolutionists of '48 brought a new element into the State. To many of them slavery was abhorrent.

"It is not to be believed that European democrats, who have suffered exile for their social theories, would at once abandon them, and, by fraternizing with an aristocracy of slave proprietors, belie here every principle for which they had struggled at home." [27]

It is noteworthy that many of the leaders of whatever movement against slavery there was, were of those coming after the late forties. Among them were two men who had an especial influence, both on the culture of the community and on politics. These were Dr. Adolf Douai, who was the first editor of the *San Antonio Zeitung,* and Dr. A. Siemering, who was the founder of the *San Antonio Frei Presse,* in 1865, and later of the *San Antonio Express.*[28] The fact that many were led to adopt the principles of the party in power through official pressure, is shown by the story noted in the *Southern Intelligencer,* of Austin, June 15, 1859. A postmaster, when asked if he were going to support Houston or Runnels, replied that Houston supported Buchanan's administration, Runnels did not. Buchanan made him postmaster.

In the German settlements where few Americans dwelt, and the number of slaves was comparatively small, there was no occasion for especial thought on the question of slavery. It was only in the cities such as San Antonio where the population was of equal proportion, that the interests of the two elements "clashed and bitter feelings" were aroused.[29] In that city in the early fifties a number of Germans raised by subscription enough money to support a local paper. This was the *Zeitung.* Dr. Adolf Douai, a prominent exile who had had literary experience, was made editor. The editor announced himself a radical Demo-

---

[27] *Texas Journeys,* p. 438.
[28] For brief sketch see Bruncken, *German Pol. Refugees,* p. 58ff; for Siemering, Armin Tenner: *Amerika, Index.*
[29] *Texas Journeys,* p. 433.

crat, "and his determination to regard every political question from the point of view of social progress."³⁰ The tone of the paper was literary and educational, but slavery, of course, could not be ignored.

"Its economical variance with the interests of the German free laborers, and with the natural future of the Western prairies, was now and then dwelt upon; and on the main question of the essential temporariness or permanence of slavery in America, involving, in national politics, extension and furtherance, or restriction and localization, the ground natural to a democrat was taken." ³¹

His topics discussing slavery circulated only among Germans, and hence the Americans took little notice of them at first. At San Antonio, May 14-16, 1854, the second annual musical festival of the Germans in Texas was held. The musical societies of that city, New Braunfels and Sisterdale, and representatives from the musical societies of Indianola, Victoria, La Grange, Coletta and Fredericksburg were present. They sang songs of love, war, religion, etc.³² On the fifteenth, a number of the men assembled and formed a political party. The *San Antonio Ledger* states that the Germans asserted that they did not intend to form a German party, but "to reject the abuses of the old party politics, the corruption of leading men and officeholders, and wished the Constitution of the United States to be really carried out.³³ The *Atlantische Studien,* of 1854, announced previously to the San Antonio convention that an organization had been formed among the Germans of Texas, and that resolutions had been adopted demanding, among other things, the gradual emancipation of slaves; that the same rights be given to the free colored men as to the whites; and the abolition of military justice in time of peace. It states that these resolutions will be discussed at the Sängerfest to be held at San Antonio in May of that year.³⁴ At the convention various resolutions were

---

³⁰ *Ibid*, p. 434.
³¹ *Ibid*.
³² *San Antonio Ledger*, May 18, 1854.
³³ *Ibid*.
³⁴ *Atlantische Studien*, 1854, p. 214.

adopted.[35] The following resolution was adopted regarding slavery:

"Slavery is an evil whose ultimate removal is, according to democratic principles, indispensable; but as it affects only individual states, we demand: that the Federal Government refrain from all interference in affairs of slavery; but that, when any single state shall resolve on the removal of this evil, the aid of the government may be claimed." [36]

The following amendments were rejected:

"Slavery is, according to our views, a social evil, and possibly liable to conflict with white labor. But this institution comes too little home to Germans and is too much connected with the interests of our American fellow citizens, for us to feel ourselves urged to take, in this question, initiatory steps, or to act upon it politically."

"Negro slavery is an evil, perilous to the duration of the Union. Its abolition must be left to the individual states in which it exists. We German-speaking Texans are not naturally in a position to initiate measures, but we wish the Federal Government's patronage of the same dispensed with." [37]

The newspapers were filled with accounts denunciatory of the convention. It furnished thunder for the "Know-Nothing" movement. The *San Antonio Herald*, a "Know-Nothing" organ, was especially denunciatory and abusive. It claimed that the Germans were plotting to form a free state in Western Texas. This question will be considered in a more detailed account later. The *San Antonio Ledger*, June 22, 1854, in announcing the resolutions of the convention, says:

"We have been disposed * * * to defend our German population against the charges of abolitionism and disposition to interfere with the laws of our country. If the above is true, we have been misled and have probably misled others. The charges are of a very serious nature." If the Germans are "engaged in forming secret societies in league with similar fanatics of the North, to undermine and uproot our institutions and laws * * * it is

---

[35] Cf. *supra*, Ch. IV, for other resolutions.

[36] This is a translation given in Olmsted, Texas Journeys, p. 435, footnote. The original was: "Die Sklaverei ist ein Uebel, dessen endliche Beseitigung, den Grundsätzen der Demokratie gemäss, nothwendig ist; da sie aber nur einzelne Staaten betrifft, so fordern wir; Dass die Bundesregierung sich aller Einmischung in Sachen der Sklaverei enthalte; dass aber, wenn ein einzelner Staat die Beseitigung dieses Uebels beschliesst, alsdann zur Ausführung dieses Beschlusses die Bundeshulfe in Anspruch genommen werden kann."

[37] *Texas Journeys*, footnote, p. 435.

time the people of the State should know it. Let any portion of our population undertake a crusade by means of secret associations or otherwise against slavery, our laws, our religion and its ministers in Texas, and they will raise a storm of indignation from which they will be glad to escape by any means within their power."

The same journal, under date of July 20, 1854, says that it was announced in a paper in Pennsylvania that the Germans were to hold a great abolition convention in San Antonio in May; that the same paper gave the number of bales of cotton raised in that section of Texas by free German labor and attempted to show that that labor was cheaper and better than slave labor. The *Ledger* continues: "If all this be true (and we do not doubt it is), it would seem that we have a branch of the underground railroad. No doubt, some of the directory reside in our city. Who knows?"

The Germans throughout the State, by means of resolutions and otherwise, hastened to deny the allegations made against them. They claimed that the singing societies met simply for singing and amusement; that Americans were not invited because they had no singing societies; that the platform of the San Antonio convention was adopted by Germans not natives of the United States; that the majority in Western Texas was opposed to the San Antonio convention.[38] A meeting of several hundred Germans was held in New Braunfels. Resolutions were proposed, in which the movement, originated by certain Germans of the North and responded to in Texas by the so-called San Antonio convention, were denounced. "It becomes our duty to assist with all good citizens in bringing such movements to an end."[39] The Washington correspondent of the *Austin Gazette* states that the abolitionists in Congress have their speeches duly translated into German and distributed under the Congressional "frank" among the Germans of Western Texas.[40]

The German paper at San Antonio was severely criticised by the newspapers of the State. It had published the resolutions

---

[38] Cf. letter dated June 27, 1854, in *Texas State Gazette*, July 8, 1854; also same paper of June 30, 1855.
[39] *Ibid*, July 29, 1854.

of the San Antonio convention and had defended them. Its editor had to bear the brunt of the accusations against that convention. Two parties were formed among the Germans. A meeting of the stockholders of the paper was called, in which Douai's course was sustained, but the paper was sold and Douai continued to publish it himself. His editorials were translated into English so that they might be read by the Americans. This aroused the fury of the papers again, and the American merchants were prevailed upon to withdraw their advertisements.[41] The *State Gazette*, under date of May 12, 1855, contained the following regarding that publication:

"The editor of the German paper avers himself opposed to slavery, we are sorry to see anything that might ultimately destroy our peace and harmony. * * * We are indeed sorry that a paper with free soil proclivities can find a resting place in Texas. If the editor of the *Zeitung* is a free soiler or an abolitionist, we would give him two alternatives, to desist from a doctrine which is to rob us of our prosperity or to take up his march."

Under date of the nineteenth of the same month, it declares:

"Were it printed in English, we do not believe that there is a respectable man in San Antonio that would not be incensed by its free soilism, and we cannot say what course might be pursued toward its proprietors."

Under date of June 22, the same periodical states that the *Zeitung* would come, in Louisiana, within the range of the statutes which provide for imprisonment for life or the infliction of the death penalty on any person who shall publish or distribute such works; that it hoped to see the Louisiana law re-enacted in Texas and carried out. Numerous conventions were held denying that the Germans were responsible for the views declared by Doctor Douai in the *San Antonio Zeitung*. One held in the Comal County Court-house in New Braunfels, illustrates the tendency of the German leaders to disclaim any views in accord with those set forth by Douai. The convention was held June 26, 1855. Resolutions were drawn up denying that the Germans of Comal County were in any way responsible for the

---

[41] Olmsted, *Texas Journeys*, p. 437.

sentiments as set forth in the *San Antonio Zeitung;* that only the individuals publishing and endorsing such resolutions should be held as sponsors.[42] At Lockhart, the Germans assembled and demanded that Douai be displaced from the editorship. The resolutions continued to state:

"We recommend to our German countrymen to discountenance and suppress attempts to disturb the institution of slavery, upon which is founded the prosperity and happiness of our Southern country; and to meet and express themselves most decidedly in regard to their true and genuine allegiance to the laws and institutions of the state which we inhabit, at a time when Northern abolitionists take as decided a stand, as to make actual aggression upon the constitutional rights and the property of our Southern states."[43]

The result of the attitude of the Americans, and the attitude later taken by the Germans, was that Douai was forced to abandon his paper and to go to the North to reside. Here he became a leader in the formation of the Republican Party, and was one of the Germans who issued at Boston a call to form a Republican organization of all Germans in the United States. He later became well known as a writer on pedagogical subjects.[44] His paper, under its new management, announced that it would advocate the principles of the Democratic Party, believing that that party was "the conservative party of the Union," and that it insured "the permanency of our great Republic."[45]

The time adopted by the radical Germans was not suited to the advancement of their ideas. It was the time when the American party was gaining in influence and was beginning to enter Texan politics. The San Antonio convention furnished them material with which to cry out against interference by foreigners in politics; the danger from them of establishing abolition ideas; nay, even, they went so far as to claim that the Germans intended to form a free State in Texas. This statement was taken up by the "Know-Nothing" papers throughout the country. The result was that many Germans joined the Democratic ranks who might

---

[42] *State Gazette,* July 11, 1855.
[43] *Ibid,* July 25, 1855.
[44] Bruncken, *Political Refugees,* p. 53ff.
[45] *San Antonio Ledger,* October 1, 1855.

otherwise have been "left out of the fold." This fact is shown by the following quotation from the *State Gazette,* of Austin:

"In no part of the South has the recent contest with Know-Nothingism more fully determined the character of the foreign population in favor of slavery than in Western Texas. A few madcaps and wild theorists among them had performed acts and enacted scenes which were greedily caught hold of by the Know-Nothings to stamp the whole German population with the charge of being abolitionists. * * * The events of the past contest called out the German population, and they avowed their Southern feelings and opinions; advocated the institution of slavery, and finally put down the free soil paper at San Antonio, called the *Zeitung,* and established in its place a sound and orthodox democratic sheet with the whole Democratic ticket at its masthead.

"The Germans of Western Texas have vindicated their character from the reproaches of Know-Nothings, and when our railroads enable them to cultivate the soil on a larger scale than at present, they will be owners of slaves." [46]

The *New Braunfels Zeitung,* of which Dr. Ferdinand Lindheimer was the editor, states that the "Know-Nothing" party has accused the Germans of Texas of not being sound states-rights men. Lindheimer repudiates the accusation and declares his views as follows:

"According to the Constitution of the Union, and the law of nations, a State may permit or exclude slavery from within her limits, and no other state can interfere with this right. For the same reason, it may be said that a territory can neither enact laws impairing the value of slaves, nor deny the right to the owner to introduce slave property before such Territory has the necessary number of inhabitants to be admitted as a sovereign State into the Union in the manner prescribed by law." [47]

The Democratic papers declared that the attitude of the "Know-Nothing" party toward foreigners was keeping immigrants from settling in Texas.[48]

The *Texas State Gazette* attributed an article copied from the *New Orleans Creole* to the *Western Texan,* in which the lat-

---

[46] *State Gazette,* May 10, 1856.
[47] Quoted from *New Braunfels Zeitung* in *State Gazette,* September 27, 1856.
[48] Cf. *State Gazette,* October 20, 1855, and *San Antonio Ledger,* December 16, 1858.

ter journal, under the heading "Western Texas a Free State," was made to say:

"Some may look upon such an event as a free State of Western Texas, as improbable, particularly at a time when such strenuous efforts are being made to carry slavery into Kansas, where slavery does not exist by positive law. Yet there is a strong probability that such an event will occur in the next ten years. Our opinion is based upon the fact that foreign immigration is greater than domestic, by at least ten to one; and upon the well known fact that all foreign immigration is opposed to slavery, from principle, prejudice and education. And there are many of the immigrants from the other states opposed to slavery, who quietly tolerate it so long as it is an institution of the State, but who will vote no slavery when the question comes up, whether Western Texas shall be free or slave State. This fact is not generally known; if so, it is not duly considered. The vote of the adopted citizens now number at least twelve thousand. In less than ten years it will be changed to three times that number, unless the naturalization laws are changed. This increase will be a much greater ratio than that of the native born vote." [49]

The *Western Texan* immediately denied this charge, and the *San Antonio Herald*, a "Know-Nothing"[50] organ, admitted that the article in question came from its columns, with the following comment:

"What doctrine is set forth in the above extract that he refuses to 'daddy'? Is it the probability that an effort will be made at no distant day, to declare Western Texas a free State? Is it the fact that foreigners are opposed to slavery, and will, almost to a man, vote for making Western Texas a free State when the question comes up? Or is it that this question will come up within the next ten years, owing to the more rapid increase of the foreign over the native vote, unless the naturalization laws are changed? He should be more explicit these suspicious times. We contend that the contents of the article are not mere speculations.

"If facts like the foregoing do not warn the people of the South, they will not be awakened 'though one rose from the dead'! It is a monstrous anomaly that while we are constantly excited by attempts to make free soil on our Western border, we exhibit no emotion as to a similar process going surely on in territory, in which the South has the deepest interest." [51]

---

[49] *State Gazette*, May 24, 1856.
[50] For Know-Nothing influence, cf. *San Antonio Ledger*, January 26, 1858.
[51] *State Gazette*, May 24, 1856. The article in the *New Orleans Creole* on which these editorials were based, was:
"A Free State out of Texas.— From various sources we have come to

The *New Orleans Picayune* says, regarding the division of Texas, that one of the principal reasons Texas has not been divided into more than one State has been the fear that one division would be a free State, because of the predominance of foreigners who are opposed to slavery. It says that that danger is over-rated, but to offset it, it is proposed to make a State out of the First Congressional District, which is pro-slavery in its sentiments.[52]

From these citations it is readily seen that this idea that the Germans intended to form a free State out of Western Texas was due to the "Know-Nothing" journals, which wished to use it as a slogan against all foreigners. It is probable that some of the more radical Germans, however, may have had such ideas in mind. Kapp states that all the Germans of Texas were abolitionists; that an immigration of from ten to twenty thousand Germans a year would soon result in forming a free State in Western Texas.[53]

The result of the "Know-Nothing" movement is shown in the returns of the German counties in the elections when it was at its height. The counties of Comal, Gillespie and Medina chose as their representative in the Texan House of Representatives, Jacob Waelder, a Northern German who was pro-slavery in his proclivities. He made the following speech in that body:

"Sir, if the citizens of German birth were not sound upon the question of slavery, I would not now probably occupy a seat upon this floor * * * I can say, sir, and I do say without the fear of successful contradiction, that the citizens of German birth re-

---

possession of facts which go to show that the Germans, French, Swiss, Hungarians and other foreigners will, ere long, make a free state out of Western Texas. We have lately conversed with men from that part of the State, and they unhesitatingly aver that the foreigners there to a man are opposed to slavery.

"There are also men from the North who are insidious leaders in the movement, and are urging the foreigners to take a bold stand in favor of the project. They are busy in the work of drilling them for the contest, and already boast of having ten thousand voters."

Cf. Olmsted, *Texas Journeys*, p. 502; also *New York Independent*, October 22, 1857. Von Holst evidently accepted as true the statements that the Germans intended to form a free state. Cf. Von Holst, Vol. VI, p. 305, footnote.

[52] From New Orleans *Picayune*, quoted in *San Antonio Ledger*, December 26, 1857.

[53] Kapp, article in *N. Y. Tribune*, January 20, 1855.

siding in the counties of Comal, Gillespie, Medina and Bexar, are in their majority neither abolitionists or free soilers, but as a body, they are as loyal to the Union and as loyal to the institutions of the South as the citizens of any section of the country, North or South." [54]

In the November elections of 1856 Comal County gave Buchanan 256 votes to 26 cast for Fillmore for President.[55] The small number of votes cast in proportion to the population is readily noticed. A number of the naturalized citizens of Fayette County, July 19, 1857, in mass-meeting assembled, resolved to vote unanimously the Democratic ticket.[56] In a Democratic meeting held at New Braunfels, Waelder was commended for his speech, and Sam. Houston was denounced as a panderer to abolitionism and free-soilism. It was recommended to their senator and representative to aid in the passage of a resolution asking him to resign.[57] It is stated that Houston said that he expected the vote of the Germans because they believed him an abolitionist.[58]

Douai, who, since his removal from Texas had been active in the interests of the Republican party, came out in the *New York Tribune* with an attack on Waelder, who had been appointed as consul to Frankfurt on the Main. He asserted that Waelder, in defending a man who had made an assault upon an anti-slavery German, stated that to kill a man who assailed the institution of slavery was no crime.[59] The *Tribune* came out with an extended editorial regarding the subject. Among other statements, it said:

"This miserable renegade has been sent to disgrace us abroad. We trust, however, the mark we thus stamp upon him will secure him repudiation in Germany, such as his conduct in America has amply deserved."[60]

Waelder later replied in June in the same paper denying Douai's assertions.

---
[54] Delivered in Texan House of Rep., November 15, 1855.
[55] *State Gazette,* November 15, 1856.
[56] *Ibid,* July 29, 1857.
[57] *Ibid,* December 29, 1855.
[58] *San Antonio Ledger,* July 25, 1857.
[59] *N. Y. Weekly Tribune,* May 9, 1857 (*San Antonio Ledger,* June 15, 1857, mentions the circumstance).
[60] *Ibid.*

The question of reviving the slave trade brought out in the *New Braunfels Zeitung* an editorial in opposition to it. On account of its arguments, and as an example of the style of Ferdinand Lindheimer's editorials, incidentally showing the character of the German Texan newspaper, it is given *in extenso:*

"We are firmly convinced that at the coming Democratic State Convention, the various views regarding the slave trade being reopened will not only be amply discussed, but will also influence the nominations. Undoubtedly, the convention will serve as a barometer indicating whether the ultra Southern or conservative side of the Slavery question will be in the ascendency. The results of these debates will be the more important as the eyes of the whole South will be fixed upon Texas. We have repeatedly demonstrated that we can see no solid reasons for the revival of the African Slave Trade. The slave trade resumed against the will and in contravention to treaties with European nations would necessarily demand the protection of an American fleet, for the support of which Congress as now composed, would never vote an appropriation, and a separation of the South from the North is not so easily accomplished. And even were the South to form a distinct republic, it could not successfully combat the maritime powers of the world in defense of the Slave Trade.

"If the measure of utility is applied to the slavery agitation as practiced both North and South by the ultras, the sad result seems to follow that on the social-political and national-economical field even where reality should pre-eminently be discussed, an unconsciencious humbug is enacted. The ultra Southerner should consider that only a possibility has a hope of realization; and the ultra Northerner, that only realities are possible. This is the position we occupy on the slavery question, unattainable, however, to many Germans, especially in the North. * * * But that the sound sense and judgment of the majority of Texian Germans inclines to neither extreme will, we doubt not, be demonstrated by the ballot box, whenever the slavery question is brought to bear in election.

"We Germans are usually rather conservative on questions of practical life, hence our greater attachment to the homestead, our parents, ancestors and customs.

"One can venture to assert that all the Germans in Texas with as rare exceptions as among Americans will repudiate the violent and unlawful means commended and used in the North against slaveholders; but neither can they or any other patriot desire that the estate of the small farmer be supplanted by millions of slaves. North and South, the small farmers are in the majority and form the heart core of the nation. Without them, the democratic character of our nation would be lost. That the self-working husbandman in the good old time of the Roman Republic was so highly esteemed; that ebriety, industry and hard labor, unlike the Greeks, was greatly esteemed: these laid the foundation of the future greatness of that Republic. But when afterwards slave labor became so cheap that not only farming and stock raising, but handicrafts and factories were carried on with slaves, the whole nation, whose frugality was proverbial, soon so degenerated that foreign hirelings had to defend it against exterior enemies; while in the interior, the impudent praetorian soldiery and most shameless abuses ruled supreme.

"Now, our slave holders are not to be looked upon as a species of landed nobility, aristocrats, negro barons and debauching nabobs, but as industrious agriculturists operating on a greater scale. But how different an aspect would the institution of slavery assume, if the favored idea of the ultra Southerners, of every farmer tilling his few acres with a couple of negroes, be realized.

"Looking upon the present conditions of slavery in the Union, as neither a wrong nor an immorality, but a rightfully existing state, yet we cannot but declare the reopening of the slave trade an impossibility, and if possible so fraught with danger to the interests and existence of these United States, and thereby to the civilized world that looks upon us as the model republic of modern times, and the grandest experiment of self-government and national welfare, that all speculations of plantation profit, negro civilization and conversion are nothing to compare to it. * * *

"We can truthfully assert that the mass of the Texian Germans are not opposed to slavery. As early as 1836, the opinion that the Southern States of the United States were a less aristocratic and more republican people than the North, prevailed among the more intelligent and highly cultivated Germans that served in the Texian army.

"I am also convinced that at the cheap price of from $100 to $200 for a negro, many a German farmer would procure one or more of those ever ready laborers, and the more so, as now frequently when needed, a laborer cannot be had at $1 per day. Still I entertain some doubts whether a general introduction of domestic slavery, especially among us Germans, who usually miss that true middle course between severity and over-indulgence, would not exert a pernicious influence upon the family life of our whites and, in particular, upon the whole bearing of our slave population.

"History is a great teacher and she tells us that not only with the nations of antiquity, but up to the present day in the Orient, domestic slavery was a hot-bed of impertinent impudence and a nursery of sedition. Some few cases excepted, the small farmer can well get along without slaves. Should they not be able to compete with the large plantations in the culture of cotton, which I, however, doubt, as American planters frequently hire German help during the picking season, and as cotton picked by Germans has proved much cleaner, there still remain many branches of industry to the industrious farmer in which he need not fear the competition of black labor—grape culture, sheep raising, tobacco planting, and fruit raising * * * Manufactures and mines will be opened and we have hundreds of Germans experienced in the arts of weaving manifold woofs, and, as regards miners, it is known to the world that the Germans excel in practice as well as in theory, all other nations, as instanced by the fact that English mines in Mexico and the rich mines of Arizona are worked and superintended by German geologists and mineralogists." [61]

Previously to the election of 1860, the German Democrats of Comal County endorsed the Democratic party, stating that they were opposed to "the Black Republican" party because it was against the Union.[62] In the State election of that year, Comal County went Democratic by a vote of 425 for the Democratic candidates, to ten votes against them; and Gillespie County went Democratic by a vote of 290 for, to 60 against that party.[63] A large number of the population must not have voted at all. These counties had a population of about 4000 and 3000, respectively, at that time.[64] In a letter dated New Braunfels, August 20 of that year, it is stated that nearly every voter is for Breckinridge and Lane.[65] One German newspaper, *Die Union,* of Galveston, however, denounced the Charleston convention and called the Texan delegates "pitiful blockheads."[66] In 1856 the same paper had stated that Congress had no right to interfere with slavery in the territories.[67] This was during the height of the "Know-Nothing" movement. That movement was dead; the danger of secession was in the air; hence the change.

When the question of secession arose, many of the Germans were strongly opposed and remained firm to the Union. Gustav Schleicher, who later became a member of the House of Representatives, worked hard to keep the State in the Union; but when his State decided to secede he thought it his duty to accept, and when the war broke out he enlisted and became an engineer

---

[61] Quoted from *New Braunfels Zeitung* in *Southern Intelligencer,* April 6, 1859.
[62] *State Gazette,* March 24, 1860.
[63] *Ibid,* August 25, 1860.
[64] Cf. Olmsted for 1856, *supra.*
[65] *State Gazette,* August 25, 1860.
[66] *Ibid,* July 14, 1860.
[67] *Ibid,* October 25, 1856.

in the Confederate army. He constructed many forts for the Confederates, notably Fort Sabine.[68] The leading men of Comal County determined to stand by the South. In a convention at New Braunfels, in December, 1860, they averred that "by the election of 'Abe' Lincoln as President of the United States, the institutions of the Southern States of our glorious Confederacy are imperiled;" they demanded that "the Governor of Texas be requested to convene the Legislature at a time as early as practicable, so that the representatives may take action in this most important cause, to call a State Convention," and state that "unless their rights and institutions are duly guaranteed by the North, we assert the right of Texas to resume peaceably or by force all the power she has delegated to the Federal Government, and we recommend the organization of our whole population for the defense of her rights."[69] These resolutions are, however, not an indication of the feeling of the majority of the population. Since the "Know-Nothing" movement, it had been with the Democratic party, now it was for the Union. They voted in favor of secession, many of them, because they feared through opposition to the great majority of the American population, to endanger their own welfare.[70] A German is said to have offered Houston 2000 Germans to break up the Secession Convention.[71] The belief in an early victory for the North prevented many German settlements from taking any decided action. In Gillespie County, in which Fredericksburg was situated, there was a secret organization in behalf of the Union, and it is stated that any member who became a traitor would have been shot at sight.[72] The Latin settlement of Sisterdale was entirely on the side of the Union. This resulted in its dissolution.[73] The majority of its members

---

[68] Koerner, p. 365.
[69] *State Gazette*, December 15, 1860.
[70] Seele, article in *Jahrbuch*, p. 32ff. Seele was secretary of the Comal convention noted, *supra*.
[71] Schem, *Conversations Lexicon*, Vol. X, p. 694.
[72] *Ibid.*
[73] Letter of Rudolf Wipprecht to the *Amerikanisches Magazine*, 1887, dated College Station, Texas, May 10, 1887.

were made up of educated men.[74] They went to Mexico, California, Germany and New York. Comal County furnished three companies for the Confederate army. These were: the company under Captain G. Hofmann, which fought in Sibley's brigade in New Mexico; the company under command of Captain Podawill, which fought in Wood's regiment; and the infantry company under command of J. Boses, which fought in Louisiana.[75] The war encouraged manufacturing in New Braunfels, as many things that were formerly imported were manufactured there.[76]

Some seventy Germans formed a military organization with the object of marching to Mexico and joining from there the Union army. They were met and attacked by a large body of Confederates at the Neuces River, August 10, 1862. Of the seventy, thirty-two were killed; some of the others were taken prisoners and later shot, and only seven escaped.[77] Many Germans were conscripted by the Confederates; hundreds crossed the Rio Grande and later enlisted in the Union army, in which they formed whole cavalry companies in the First Texan Regiment.[78]

During the reconstruction period the Germans joined the Republican party en masse. In the Reconstruction Convention, many were prominent participants; among them Degner, who, in 1869 was chosen to the United States House of Representatives; Knechler, who, the same year, became General Land Commissioner of the State, and Julius Schuetze, who for many years was editor of a leading German paper. In the State Legislature of 1870, three Germans were senators and seven representatives; in that of 1872, five were representatives, and one a senator.[79]

---

[74] Kapp, *Aus und über Amerika*, p. 287ff.
[75] Seele in *Jahrbuch für Texas*.
[76] *Ibid.*
[77] Schem, Vol. X, p. 694ff.
[78] *Ibid.*
[79] *Ibid.*

CHAPTER VI.

ELEMENTS OF CULTURE.

SCHOOLS, NEWSPAPERS, SINGING SOCIETIES AND SOCIETIES FOR INTELLECTUAL IMPROVEMENT, LITERATURE, RELIGION, EXAMPLES OF CULTURED GERMANS.

Even during the earliest days of the German settlements in Texas, the elements which go to make up civilized and cultured communities were introduced. Schools, singing societies, various societies for intellectual improvement, and well edited newspapers were common in those communities which were large enough to warrant their introduction. The fact that so large a portion of the population consisted of men with some claims to culture aided in establishing such institutions. There were probably in the South few communities of like size that could show schools of such a character or newspapers discussing topics of so varied an interest, as the small German communities of Western Texas. The Verein in its program had promised the introduction of schools and the building of churches, at the association's cost, as soon as the population should be large enough to permit such additional expense. The "forty-eighters" introduced a valuable element into the society of Texas. Settlements such as the "Latin Colony" at Sisterdale, and the "Communistic Colony of Bettina," were comprised almost exclusively of men of culture. Some of the latter, better known as "Men of the Forties," such as Gustav Schleicher and Doctor Ferdinand Herff, became leaders in the political and intellectual life of the State. Nearly all writers who visited the various communities recognize the exceptional culture of their inhabitants. Kapp found in those districts, far from any thickly populated settlements, and even in those which were in the territory of the Indians, German settlements which had their "Reading Clubs" and "Periodical Clubs," in which they kept abreast with the latest German literature. In many log-houses he found settlers who possessed copies of the

German classic poets. In the same communities, the more recent works on economics, history and philosophy were found shortly after their publication.[1] Froebel notes the fact, in reference to Castro's colony, that those German settlements were especially interesting for the civilization which they have brought into the wilderness,[2] a fact which has "struck all Anglo-American travellers."[3]

EDUCATION.

As noted above, the Eighth Congress of the Texan Republic incorporated, in 1842, an institution to be known as Hermann University. L. C. Ervendberg, F. Ernst, H. Schmidt, H. Amthor, J. G. Sieper, C. Stoehr, F. W. Huesmann and F. Frank were made the first board of trustees. This institution was to consist of law, medical, theological and philosophical departments. Preparatory schools were to be established in connection with the institution proper. No person could be appointed to any professorship unless he understood both the English and the German languages, unless such qualifications were disregarded by a unanimous vote of the trustees. The institution was not allowed to establish any religious qualification in order to become a trustee, professor, instructor or student. The theological faculty could not be styled by any particular religious denomination. It was to be known as "the Protestant Faculty." A league of public land was set aside for the use of the university.[4]

In August, 1845, shortly after the colony of New Braunfels was established, a school was opened. This, at first, was a private school.[5] The first German pastor, L. C. Ervendberg, kept a private school in which he gave instruction in the classics.[6] In 1850 Comal County had three schools, with four teachers and 130 pupils; Gillespie County had four schools, with six teachers and 137 pupils; Medina County, two schools, with two teachers

---

[1] Kapp, *Aus and über Amerika*, Pt. II, p. 287.
[2] Froebel, *Central America*, p. 423.
[3] *Ibid.*
[4] Gammel, *Laws of Texas*, Vol. II, p. 948ff.
[5] *Jahrbuch*, p. 32ff.
[6] *Texas Journeys*, p. 172.

and twenty-seven pupils.⁷ When Olmsted visited New Braunfels, there were in that town and the surrounding country five free schools for elementary education, one Roman Catholic school, a town free school of higher grade, and a private classical school. In all of the schools English and German were both taught.⁸ In 1850 there were in Gillespie County no persons, according to the census of that year, who could not read or write; in Comal County there were thirteen illiterates; and in Medina County, fourteen. That there were so few who could not read or write is accounted for from the fact that there were so few negroes in those counties. In New Braunfels, in the fifties, in the high school, American as well as German teachers were employed. Instruction was given in the classics, natural history and higher mathematics.⁹ At San Antonio there was a school, established by German influence, in which there were teachers from Harvard.¹⁰ In 1846 a German school was established at Galveston. It was made an occasion for a celebration, and a description was published ¹¹ in the Northern papers. In 1860 the New Braunfels Academy was incorporated. That city was the first in Texas to support a public school through taxation.¹² The provisions of the Texan Constitution, by which cities and towns are authorized to tax themselves for the purpose of schools, were embodied in that document at the suggestion of a citizen of Comal County; and the law carrying the provisions into effect was introduced by the representative of that county.¹³ At that time New Braunfels had 250 pupils who did not pay any tuition fee.¹⁴ In 1870 Comal County had 157 who could not read or write, out of a population of about 5000;¹⁵ Gillespie, 57 illiterates out of a population of

---

⁷ *Census of 1850*, p. 508.
⁸ *Texas Journeys*, p. 179.
⁹ *Cotton Kingdom*, II, p. 103.
¹⁰ *Ibid*.
¹¹ Koerner, p. 365.
¹² *Texas Almanac*, 1861, p. 191; also Seele, *Short History of Comal County*.
¹³ Seele, Hermann, *Short History of Comal County*.
¹⁴ *Texas Almanac*, 1861, p. 191.
¹⁵ According to *Texas Almanac* for 1871, Comal County had 10,000. If

3500. These two counties were almost exclusively German in population. Austin County, in which the capital of the State was located, at that time had 674 illiterates out of a population of 15,000.[16] These statistics are based on the white population. They do not include the number of negroes. In other words, Austin County, located in the centre of the white population, had almost five per cent. of its white population illiterate, while Comal County, which was further west, only had three per cent., and Gillespie, which was near the western border, had a little over three per cent. It would not be fair to carry this estimate later, as it would be difficult to say how many Americans were in those counties at a later period. In 1871, New Braunfels, with a' population of 5000, had in its Academy some four to five hundred students. German and English were both taught. There were some three or four other schools in the town.[17] As late as 1871 there were very few public schools in the various towns of Texas. Private schools were the most common, although there were some free elementary schools. This fact speaks well for the educational condition of New Braunfels, when we consider that as early as 1860 it made all of its schools absolutely free, supported by taxation and the school funds of the State. The Germans early established private schools where both English and German were taught. In 1882, nineteen places in Texas, with 84 teachers and 3193 pupils were supported by Germans. These were known as the German-English schools, and did not include the parochial or denominational schools.[18]

NEWSPAPERS.

Newspapers were established early in the German communities. Their character was beyond the ordinary. In 1847, *Die Union* was established at Galveston.[19] During the "Know-Nothing" movement, it was extremely pro-slavery in sentiment. It

---

this be true, the percentage of illiterates for 1870 would be decreased considerably in Comal County.

[16] *Census of* 1870.
[17] *Texas Almanac*, 1871, p. 102.
[18] Tenner, Armin, *Amerika, Index—Texas*.
[19] Wooten, B. G., *Comprehensive History of Texas*, Vol. II, p. 392.

repudiated the Charleston Convention [20] and was accused of being weak-kneed by the American Democratic press of the State. The *Zeitung,* in San Antonio, was established in 1853,[21] with Dr. Adolf Douai as its first editor. Its character was of a high order. Olmsted says that he found it contained more news of general interest than all the American newspapers in Texas.[22] On November 30, 1852, the *New Braunfels Zeitung* was founded by Dr. Ferdinand Lindheimer.[23] Lindheimer was a strong Democrat. He opposed the Germans, who remained in the majority, loyal to the Union.[24] He often opposed the Confederates and might have been harmed but for his known courage. The character of his editorials has alrady been described. They showed a grasp of public questions and a knowledge of history which few of the contemporary papers of the country could have furnished. In 1904 there were twenty-nine newspapers published in Texas.[25] These were:

Austin, *Texas Vorwärts,* 21st year of publication, weekly.
Austin, *Schuetze's Monatsbuch für Texas,* 1st year of publication, monthly (discontinued with death of the publisher in 1905.).
Belleville, *Wochenblatt,* 14th year, weekly.
Brenham, *Volksbote,* 31st year, weekly.
" *Lutherischer Gemeindebote für Texas,* 13th year, semi-monthly.
Cuero, *Deutsche Rundschau,* 13th year, semi-weekly.
Dallas, *Feld und Flur,* 6th year, monthly.
" *Nord Texas Presse,* 13th year, semi-weekly.
Fredericksburg, *Deutsch-Texanische Monatshefte,* 9th year, monthly. (This is now published in San Antonio.)
Fort Worth, *Anzeiger,* 15th year, weekly.
Gainesville, *Anzeiger,* 9th year, weekly.
Galveston, *Die Galveston Post,* 2d year, weekly.
Giddings, *Deutsche Wochenblatt,* 5th year, weekly.
Gonzales, *Der Herold,* 1st year, weekly.
Hallettsville, *Lavacca County Nachrichten,* 9th year, weekly.
Houston, *Texas Deutsche Zeitung,* 31st year, weekly.
La Grange, *Deutsche Zeitung,* 15th year.

---
[20] Cf. article in *Austin Gazette,* July 4, 1860.
[21] *Ibid.*
[22] *Texas Journeys,* p. 132ff.
[23] Koerner, p. 364.
[24] *Ibid.*
[25] *Monatsbuch für Texas,* Austin, September, 1904.

New Braunfels, *Zeitung,* 52d year, weekly.
Rosebud, *Central Texas Volksblatt Zeitung,* 4th year.
San Antonio, *Freie Presse für Texas,* 40th year, daily and weekly.
San Antonio, *Katholische Rundschau,* 7th year, weekly.
" " *Texas Banner,* 1st year, weekly.
" " *Texas Staatszeitung,* 14th year, weekly.
Seguin, *Zeitung,* 14th year, weekly.
Shiner, *Shiner Rundschau,* 4th year, weekly.
Shovel, Mount, *Der Hermann Sohn in Texas,* monthly.
Taylor, *Herold,* 10th year, weekly.
Victoria, *Deutsche Zeitung für Texas,* 22d year, weekly.
Waco, *Post,* 13th year, weekly.

There are few States in the Union which have so many and so well edited German newspapers.

SOCIETIES.

The Germans had many clubs and societies, which exerted a decided cultural influence. When Olmsted visited New Braunfels, there were an Agricultural Society, a Mechanics' Institute, a Society for Political Debates, a Harmonic Society, and a Turner Society. A horticultural club had expended $1200 in one year in introducing trees and plants.[26] Olmsted says regarding these societies that they were "the evidence of an active intellectual life and desire for knowledge and improvement among the masses of the people, like that which distinguishes the New Englanders, and is unknown wherever slavery degrades labor."[27] In 1845, the first year of the settlement, a singing club was organized at New Braunfels, and one of the first songs sung was composed by Prince Solms-Braunfels.[28] During the same year, a male quartet was formed and, during the evenings, singing was indulged in by the entire settlement.[29] In 1847 New Braunfels had a good band.[30] On March 2, 1850, at that place, was formed the "Gesangverein Germania," with G. T. Peckmecky as its first director. Under its auspices the first public holiday was celebrated

---

[26] *Texas Journeys,* p. 179.
[27] *Ibid.*
[28] *San Antonio Express,* October 4, 1903.
[29] *Jahrbuch für Texas,* p. 32ff.
[30] Bracht, p. 115.

at New Braunfels.[31] At Fredericksburg, which was founded in 1846, a male quartet was formed in 1850. This was the nucleus of the later Gesangverein. Among those who were members of this society were: Frank Van der Stucken, father of the later composer of the same name, and Dr. A. Siemering, later founder and editor of the *San Antonio Express*. The members of the various societies formed a dramatic club under whose auspices Schiller's *Wallenstein* and Wagner's *Tannhäuser* were produced in the early fifties.[32] At Austin the "Maennerchor" was formed in 1853.[33] The "Germania" at New Braunfels was the nucleus for similar organizations throughout Western Texas. Its meetings were held in an open-air pavilion on the Guadaloupe River. On July 4, 1853, that society entertained singers from San Antonio and Austin, and it was then determined to call a meeting to organize a Sängerbund in Western Texas. A call was sent out accordingly, and on October 15-16, 1853, a Saengerfest was held at New Braunfels in which societies from Austin, San Antonio, Sisterdale and New Braunfels participated.[34] During the festival, a Verein was established which had for its purpose a union of all the singing societies in Texas.[35] The Saengerfeste were occasions also for expressions of political ideas. At this meeting, the representatives of the German counties in the Legislature were requested to prevent the passage of any law by which the German language should be prohibited from being taught in the public schools.[36] The Saengerfest held at San Antonio in May, 1854, has been previously described. During that year a dramatic society was formed at New Braunfels.[37] In May, 1855, the third Saengerfest was held at New Braunfels. The societies of that city, Austin, Indianola, Columbus, La Grange, Sisterdale and San Antonio were participants. The dramatic society at New Braunfels gave a play during the Saengerfest. Saenger-

---

[31] Seele, *Jahrbuch für Texas*, p. 32ff.
[32] *Fest-Ausgabe*, p. 78.
[33] Letter to Julius Schuetze, February 12, 1904.
[34] *San Antonio Express*, October 4, 1903.
[35] *Jahrbuch für Texas*, article by Seele, p. 42.
[36] *Ibid.*
[37] *Ibid.*

feste were held from that time on until the war.³⁸ After the war, the Saengerbund was revived and is still active. It holds a festival every two years, at which the various singing societies of the State are present.³⁹ This organization was divided into smaller associations, so that the smaller settlements get the benefit from the meeting of the singing societies. In October, 1881, the "Gebirgssaengerbund von West Texas" was established in the small settlement of Boerne, which was founded in 1852. During the Saengerfest held at that time, the following societies participated: "Concordia," from Fredericksburg; "Walhalla," from Comal County; "Echo," from Anhalt; "Liedertafel," from Comfort;"Concordia," from Kerrville;"Maennerchor," from Aufnau; "Gesangverein" and "Gemischter Chor," from Boerne. The program consisted of some nineteen numbers. Three male choruses sang the *Bundeslied* from Mozart; the *Jaegers Abschied,* from Mendelsohn and the *Vaterlandslied,* from Marschner. These different societies held their meetings in their various settlements under difficult conditions. The majority of the members came from the country districts and, in order to attend the various meetings during the year, had to travel ten to fifteen miles and return. All those taking part in the Saengerfest were descendants of old settlers. There were no professional musicians among them.⁴⁰ In October, 1903, the fiftieth anniversary of the German Texan Saengerbund was celebrated at New Braunfels. Judge Julius Schuetze, who was one of the founders of the original Saengerfest, was present on this occasion and delivered the oration. At the original meeting in New Braunfels in 1853, he travelled eighty miles on horseback in order to attend.⁴¹ Some 6000 to 7500 Germans were present at this reunion. San Antonio societies, consisting of the "Beethoven Maennerchor," the "Liederkranz," and the "San Antonio Maennerchor;" the Houston "Saengerbund;" Austin "Saengerbund;" the La Grange

---

³⁸ *Ibid.*
³⁹ Letter of Julius Schuetze, founder of Texan Saengerfest, February 12, 1904.
⁴⁰ *Deutsche Pionier,* Vol. XIII, No. 9, p. 368.
⁴¹ Letter of Schuetze, *supra.*

society, "Die Froesche;" besides societies from New Braunfels and other German settlements, participated.[42] On February 10, 1904, the Austin "Saengerrunde" celebrated its twenty-fifth anniversary.[43]

The May festivals which are so common in Texas have been attributed to the influence of the Germans. Siemering states that in the early eighties there was a veritable mania in Texas for "Maifeste;" that every German settlement, however small, had its annual celebration.[44]

During the fifties, in San Antonio, the Germans constructed a building for a common meeting place. In this were held the meetings of the singing societies and the dramatic associations. These societies did as much as any one thing to draw the German and American elements together. The "German Society" which constructed this building came to be "considered a central point of life" in that city.[45]

That these various associations of the Germans, especially in the small settlements at a distance from the large cities, their singing societies and dramatic clubs which often produce some of the compositions of the best dramatists and composers, have and are still exerting an important cultural influence, is quite evident.

LITERATURE.

The Germans in Texas have produced a literature, some of which, at least, is more than of an ephemeral value. Many of the German newspapers were edited by men of unusual culture. Siemering was not only the founder in San Antonio of the *Freie Presse,* but also of an American paper, *The Express.* He has published a novel dealing with the experiences of the Germans during the Civil War. The story is based on actual characters and experiences of the Germans during that period. It was called *Ein Verlebtes Leben.*[46]

---

[42] *San Antonio Express,* October 5, 1903.
[43] Letter of Schuetze, *supra.*
[44] Article by Siemering, *Deutsche Pionier,* Vol. XIV, No. 2, p. 79.
[45] *San Antonio Ledger,* February 27, 1858.
[46] A. Siemering, *Ein Verlebtes Leben,* San Antonio, 1876.

On February 14, 1882, there died a former member of the "Adelscolonie," Albert von Halfern, who had been a prolific writer. He had been a captain of Texas "Rangers" in the Mexican War and was for many years a captain in the United States army. He was the author of stories treating of his experiences among the Indians and of his army life. Among his works were: *Der Letzte der Seminolen,* scenes from the wars of the Indians of Florida with the whites; *Der Squire, Ein Bild aus den Hinterwaeldern Amerikas,* Hamburg, 1857; and *Das Leben der Indianer Nordamerikas,* Leipzig, 1863, which was his chief work.[47]

Much poetry has been produced by the Germans, although most of it is only of a transitory nature. L. F. La Frentz, the editor of *Deutsch-Texanische Monatshefte,* of San Antonio, has written many poems. His best known poem is *Am Neuces,* celebrating the occasion on which the German Union troops, in 1862, were attacked by a body of Confederates. One stanza reads as follows:

> "Vergessen sind des Krieges Greu'l, es ruft
> 'Treu der Union!' dem Norden gleich der Süden,
> In Sonnenstrahl und Blumen prangt die Gruft,
> Und über ihr, versöhnend, schwebt der Frieden."

His poem written in honor of the semi-centennial of Comfort, Texas, contains verses which are real lyrics.[48] The following description of pioneer life is an example of his style:

> "Und mit frischen, mut'gen Streben
> Geht es an die Arbeit nun,
> Dass sich Häuser bald erheben,
> Hat ein jeder flink zu tun.
> Die Zypresse, sie muss fallen,
> Dass die Schindel deckt das Haus,
> Und die deutschen Lieder schallen
> Fröhlich in den Wald hinaus.
> Möge euch das Werk gelingen,
> Wack're Kämpfer der Kultur,
> Die hier ihren Segen bringen,
> In die wilde Urnatur."

---

[47] *Deutsche Pionier,* Vol. XIV, No. 5, p. 197.
[48] Lohmann, F. H., *Comfort.*

The following is an example of his patriotic verse:

"Schlaft sanft, im Schatten eurer Eichen,
Ihr Schläfer, nach der blut'gen Schlacht,
Auf eurem Grab als Siegeszeichen
Erglänzt der Friedenspalme Pracht.

"Vorbei der Kampf! Vorbei die Rache!
Das Sternenbanner hat gesiegt!
Und die ihr fielt in heil'ger Sache,
Nun auch in seinem Schatten liegt.

"Um Einheit habt ihr ja vergossen,
Das Blut, das schmerzlich wir beweint,
Doch nicht umsonst ist es geflossen,
Seht! Nord und Süden steh'n vereint."

Goldbeck, in his work *Seit fünfzig Jahren, Prosa in Versen,* has one or two good poems. The rest, written to describe the early life of the colonists during the critical years from 1845 to 1846, are made for the occasion. The following reminds one somewhat of Goethe's *Kennt Ihr das Land,* etc.:

"Kennt ihr im fernen Süden
Das schöne Präirieland?
Es dehnet seine Fluren
Bis weit zum Rio Grand!"

"Hier blüht und duftet prächtig
Der wilde Blumenflor,
Wo aus den hohen Gräsern,
Schaut keck der Hirsch hervor."

"Der Präriehahn, der feiste
Ruft laut sein Volk herbei,
Vornehmlich in der Frühe
Ertönt sein Lockgeschrei.

"Die ungezählten Heerden
Der Farmer weiden hier,
Man hört't der Rinder Brüllen,
Der Rosse hell Gewieh'r."

" 'Fata Morgana' täuschet,
Den Wanderer oftmals sehr,
Jetzt taucht ein dunk'les Wäldchen,
Dort aus dem Gräsermeer."

Conrad Nies, the German-American poet, lived for a time in Texas, and has written several poems describing life in that State in his work, *Aus westlichen Weiten*. Although he cannot be called a Texan-German poet, the life among the Germans in that State has inspired him to some of his best lyrics. His poems, *Unter Texanischer Sonne* and *Texanischer Ostertag*, show merit. He has also written a poem dealing with the early Germans in Texas, entitled *Industry*. From *Unter Texanische Sonne*, we quote the following:

> "Texanischer Frühling durch's Bergland ging,
> Ein Wehen und Werben den Wald umfing.
> Dem deutschen Siedler ritt ich zur Seit'
> Durch die weite, blühende Einsamkeit.
>
> "Er hatte einst drüben das Schwert geführt,
> Eh' texanischen Grund sein Fuss berührt;
> Noch hatte das Tagwerk des Rangers nicht
> Den Adel geraubt dem Rassengesicht.
>
> "In seinem Auge, das blau und tief,
> Ein Abglanz versunk'ner Sonnen schlief,
> Aus Stirn und Nacken, gebräunt und breit,
> Sprach unverwüstliche Vornehmheit."

Many of the poems of the Germans have been contributed for special occasions, and so have little spontaneity; but even in these will be found occasional verses of a high order.

RELIGION.

In religion, the majority of the German settlements were Lutheran, although there were many German Catholics in Texas. Hermann University, the college founded by the early Germans, was to be Protestant in its religious character. The earliest German minister in Texas was Louis C. Ervendberg. He came to Houston, Texas, from Illinois, in 1839 and in that city established the first German Protestant Society which had 30 members and 58 who attended. From here, he founded societies at Industry with 19 members; at Cat Spring, with 29; at Biegeland, with 12; at La Grange, with 6; and at Columbus, with 6 members. Dr. Joseph A. Fischer, a professor of theology from Switzerland, was associated with him.[49] The Verein, in its program, had promised that churches would be established under its auspices, and when Solms Braunfels landed in Texas with the first colonists, he invited Ervendberg to become their pastor. The latter came to Indian Point, Christams, 1844, and when New Braunfels was founded, he became the pastor there. In October, 1845, a German Protestant society was established, and in March, 1846, a church was built. Ervendberg remained the pastor there for a number of years. Both Roemer and Olmsted speak of his simple but beautiful character.[50] During the days of 1846-7, when so many immigrants lost their lives, he established in New Braunfels an orphan asylum. He collected sixty of the children of immigrants and supported them by *farming*. During Olmsted's visit, he had still eighteen under his charge.[51] In 1847 the Verein established a church in Fredericksburg. Services were held in it by Catholics and Protestants alike. According to Roemer, there were two Catholic churches during the forties in Texas, those at Galveston and San Antonio. The Catholics in Texas were in charge of Bishop Odin. Roemer describes him as living in the simple manner of the Apostles.[52] He was respected by Protestants as well as by his own people. He ministered alike to both.

With the Revolution of 1848, a new element was introduced into the German population. It brought with it the radical tendencies then prevalent in Germany. The San Antonio Convention of May, 1854, is an example of the ideas of this new element. It was radical and rationalistic in character. Kapp, Olmsted and Mgebroff mention the rationalistic tendencies of the German population. Olmsted says:

"The virtues I have ascribed to them as a class, are not, however, without the relief of faults, the most prominent of which are a free thinking and a devotion to reason, carried, in their turn, to the verge of bigotry." [53]

---

[49] For the above, Cf. *Mgebroff*, p. 8ff.
[50] Cf. Roemer, p. 120; Olmsted, *Texas Journeys*, p. 172.
[51] *Texas Journeys*, p. 172.
[52] Roemer, p. 237.
[53] *Texas Journeys*, p .430.

On November 1, 1841, at Industry, the German Protestant churches united and formed "The United Christian Churches of Germans in Texas and the United States." A constitution was drawn up, and articles of belief, which were to be common to all, were adopted. Among these were the following: that the Holy Scriptures and the Apostolic symbols should be accepted by all; that no single belief should be considered superior, only the essentials of Christianity should be deemed necessary; a synod was to be formed, in which two ministers and two lay members, together with a president, should be a standing committee to carry on business; there should be a general synod, and a synod in each county or large division of land; this synod was to have power to decide all differences of belief or worship; the ministers of the various German churches bound themselves to perform ministerial services for all Germans. This constitution was signed by Dr. Joseph A. Fischer as President of the Synod and by Louis C. Ervendberg as Secretary.[54]

There were in 1902 in the German Lutheran churches in Texas, 12,221 communicants, and they possessed property, valued at $102,100.[55] There were in 1892 1,791 German Catholice families in Texas.[56] If we reckon three members to each family, there would be some 5,000 German Catholics in that State. The earliest German Catholic Church was that at Castroville, established in 1847.[57] The majority of Castro's settlements were Catholic.

EXAMPLES OF CULTURED GERMANS.

There are two men who deserve special mention as examples of culture among the Germans of Texas. These are Gustav Schleicher and Frank van der Stucken. The former was born at Darmstadt, Germany, November 19, 1823. He studied civil engineering at Giessen. He helped to build the railroad connecting the cities of Heidelberg and Frankfurt-on-the

---

[54] Kordül, p. 101ff.
[55] *Mgebroff*, p. 328ff.
[56] Enzlberger, Johannes, *Catholische Geistlichkeit der deutschen Zunge in den Vereinigten Staaten* (Appendix). Milwaukee, 1892.
[57] *Ibid.*

Main. He emigrated to Texas in 1847, in company with thirty-nine young and educated Germans, and settled on the Western frontier. He was one of the leading spirits in the "Communistic Colony of Bettina," better known as the "Colony of Forty" or the "Darmstaedter Kolonie." This colony soon disbanded, and in 1850 Schleicher settled in San Antonio. He became a student of the English and Spanish languages, and in 1853, was elected to the Texan House of Representatives. In 1859, he was elected as Senator from Bexar County, and served until 1861, when he entered the Confederate army as captain in the engineer corps, in which service he remained until the close of the war. After the war, he practiced engineering and was entrusted with the construction of the road from Victoria to Cuero by the Gulf and Western Texas Railroad Company. In 1874 he was elected to the Forty-fourth Congress, re-elected to the Forty-fifth and again to the Forty-sixth. He died in Washington, January 10, 1879. His colleagues recognized him as a man of unusual ability, of sterling character, and a deep student of political affairs. James A. Garfield, who was a colleague of Schleicher's in the House, declared that he had "the habit of close, earnest, hard work," and "possessed and exhibited a noteworthy independence of character." Former Secretary of State Bayard, at that time a member of the Senate, said that Schleicher gave "abundant evidence of his capacity thoroughly to examine public questions with the eye of a statesman, the labors of a scholar, and the honesty of a patriot." Bayard further states that many persons had often said to him that Schleicher would have made an admirable Cabinet officer.[58]

The latter of these two men, Frank van der Stucken, had his career in an entirely different field of activity. He was born at Fredericksburg, Gillespie County, Texas, October 15, 1858, and was the oldest son of Frank van der Stucken, a storekeeper of that place. From 1866 to 1884, he studied in Europe. Among his teachers was Benoit, of the Conservatory of Music at Antwerp. During 1877-79 he studied at Leipzig and came

---

[58] For biographical notices of Schleicher, cf. *Memorial Addresses;* also Koerner, p. 365ff.

into relationship with Edvard Grieg and Karl Reinecke. In 1881, he became Kapellmeister of the Stadt Theater at Breslau and while there conducted his own composition, the music for Shakespeare's *Tempest*. During the summer of 1883, he lived with Edvard Grieg at Rudolstadt, and there came to know Franz Liszt. During the same year, he was invited to become the director of the singing society "Arion" of New York, with which, some years later he made a journey through Europe. Since 1895, he has been the conductor of the Symphony Orchestra of Cincinnati. He has been a frequent composer of music, and as a musical director, he has been compared with Thomas, Seidl and Damrosch.[59]

---

[59] For biographical notice, cf. *Fest-Ausgabe*, p. 179; also *Who's Who in America*, 1906.

CHAPTER VII.

RELATIONS WITH THE INDIANS.
BRIEF ACCOUNT OF THE SMALLER GERMAN SETTLEMENTS.

In 1846 the United States Government signed a treaty with the Indians in Texas. By this treaty the United States was to have the sole right to regulate trade with the Indians; no traders were to be permitted among them without special permission; the Indian chiefs acknowledged themselves to be under the protection of the Government of the United States; trading posts and schools were to be established; and presents to the amount of $10,000 were to be distributed among the Indians.[1] In 1847, Congress appropriated $20,000 to carry this treaty into effect and a special agent and two interpreters were to be sent to the Indians.[2]

As for the Germans, they had friendly relations with the Indians from their earliest settlement in Western Texas. Solms Braunsfels, soon after purchasing the land for the settlement of New Braunfels, made a treaty with the Lipans in order that that territory might be settled.[3] When the Germans made their settlement at Fredericksburg in 1846, the Indians furnished them with food, and later a lucrative trade arose between the two.[4] The Indians preferred the Germans to the Americans, because the former settled in towns and villages and did not scatter over the country and kill the game, as the latter did.[5]

In order to settle the territory obtained by the Fischer and Miller grants, Meusebach determined to visit the Indians and make a treaty with them. The Texan Government refused to aid the Germans in any way in their relations with the Indians. Meusebach sent one of his officials, with twenty com-

---

[1] *United States Statutes at Large,* Vol. 9, p. 844ff.
[2] *Ibid,* p. 204.
[3] Seele, *History of Comal County.*
[4] *Texas Journeys,* p. 297.
[5] *Houston Telegraph,* May 10, 1847.

panions, to visit the territory of the Indians. This official brought back the news that there were from 40,000 to 60,000 Indians between the Llano and the San Saba.[6] Meusebach, therefore, determined to visit the Indian country himself, and by January 22, 1847, all arrangements were completed for the journey. The company consisted of a troop of cavalry, many volunteers, and forty-one American surveyors. Later, the company was joined by Major Neighbors, the Indian Agent of the United States Government, and an Indian interpreter, "Jim Shaw." On February 7, they came upon the Indian camp. Meusebach's men threw their weapons away as they were asked by the Indians to do and pitched their camp across the river from them. Many of the Indians, however, camped with them. Major Neighbors appeared and forbade Meusebach from making any treaty with the Indians and ordered him to turn back. This Meusebach refused to do, but permitted the Indian Agent to accompany him. During the same month, they met with Santa Anna, the great chieftain of the Comanches. On March 1, 1847, a treaty was discussed between the Indians and the Germans; Santa Anna, Buffalo Hump and many of the leading chiefs taking part in the councils. By the treaty, the Comanches promised the Germans that they could settle in the Indian country; and said that they would protect them from horse stealing and from other tribes; that they would permit the land to be surveyed by the Germans, and the boundaries between the Germans and the Comanches were to be specified later, the Germans promising the Indians succor in the German settlements. The treaty was to be ratified at a council to be held later at Fredericksburg, and a thousand dollars was to be paid in presents to the Indians. In his speech to the Indians, Meusebach even went so far as to say that the two races might intermarry.[7]

---

[6] This account is based on one by two German officers who accompanied Meusebach on his journey into the Indian country. It will be found in *Magazin für die Literatur des Auslandes*, 1847, p. 402ff; and also in *Fest-Ausgabe*, p. 86ff; also an account by Roemer, p. 283ff. Roemer accompanied Meusebach, and in his book publishes a diary of the journey. Soergel, *Neuste Nachrichten*, p. 113ff, has also an account of Meusebach's relations with the Indians.

[7] The speeches and treaty are given in full in *Magazin für die Literatur des Auslandes*, 1847.

On May 10, 1847, the council was to be held at Fredericksburg, where proposals were again to be made to the Indians.[8] The treaty was ratified at a meeting early in June of that year. The Indians agreed to permit the German colonists to survey the land and form any settlements that they might desire, reserving for themselves the right to hunt within the limits of the territory. Several hundred dollars' worth of presents were distributed among the Indians and it was agreed that two thousand dollars in presents were to be given to the chiefs.[9] The Comanches, according to agreement, permitted the Germans to survey the territory and became very friendly disposed toward them.[10] The *Houston Telegraph* states, September 6, 1847, that the Indians had in no way molested the Germans at Fredericksburg. Later, the Darmstaedter Colony and numerous small settlements were established among the Indians without any interference by them. The Germans, moreover, gained a very lucrative trade with them, and friendly relations seemed to be firmly established between the two races.[11] Spies, who was successor to Meusebach, declared that the Germans had spent $10,000 in cash from the Verein's funds in order to keep the friendship between the Germans and the Indians.[12] During the late fifties, the Indians made several incursions into the territory of the Germans near Fredericksburg. At the time of the twenty-fifth anniversary of the settlement of New Braunsfels, however, it was stated that that town had not been troubled by Indians for fifteen years.[14]

BRIEF ACCOUNT OF SMALLER GERMAN SETTLEMENTS.

A few of the smaller German settlements should have at least passing notice. The settlements founded by Henri Castro,

---

[8] *Houston Telegraph*, May 10, 1847.
[9] *Ibid*, June 7, 1847.
[10] *Ibid*, June 14, 1847.
[11] Cf. Account in *Fest Ausgabe*, p. 119.
[12] Letter of Spies, *Ibid*, October 28, 1847.
[13] Cf. *Accounts Texas State Gazette*, September 22, September 29, and October 6, 1855.
[14] *Deutsche Pionier*, Vol. I, p. 282.

a former soldier in the armies of Napoleon, were mainly French, although there were many Germans among them.[15] Castro received, in 1842, from the Republic of Texas, two grants of land, one of which was never settled. The other, west of San Antonio, including that portion of the country, now comprising part of Medina, Uvalde, Frio, Atascoso, Bexar, McMullen, La Salle and Zuval Counties, was settled.

In February, 1843, when Castro brought his first colonists to the City of San Antonio, no settlement existed west of the San Pedro Creek as far as the Rio Grande.

Castro published in Europe, under his own name and that of others, several pamphlets which caused Texas to become well known throughout France, Germany and Switzerland. Some of these pamphlets were *Coup d'Oeil sur Texas*, signed by Henri Fournel, published in Paris, 1841; *Documents on Foreign Commerce*, published by the Minister of Commerce in France; *Texas in 1845*, by Henry Castro, and *The State of Texas*, published at Antwerp in 1846. Many of these were translated into German.

Castro brought over to Texas from 1842 to 1847, 5,200 persons in twenty-seven ships.[16]

He left San Antonio, September 1, 1844, at the head of his colonists and established his first settlement on the Medina river, twenty-five miles west of San Antonio. This settlement was named Castroville. To-day, it is the county seat of Medina County. In 1845, an agent of Castro's founded the town of Quihi, ten miles from Castroville; and in 1846, Castro founded Vandenberg, seven miles from Quihi. In 1847, the town of Dhanis was laid out twenty-five miles still further west. These towns were, in 1871, in a flourishing condition. Castro planned to found two more towns and to surround his grant with villages. In order to establish his colonies, he had to surmount many difficulties. In 1844, he had to pay for transportation $3.50

---

[15] Cf. Koerner, p. 359; also *Texas Journeys*, p. 276ff; also *Texas State Gazette*, September 6, 1856; Mgebroff, p. 3ff; Froebel, p. 423ff; Bracht, p. 149ff.

[16] This account is based on Castro, Henri, *Texas Anvers*, 1845; and Castro, Lorenzo, *Immigration from Alsace and Lorraine*, New York, 1871. In the latter work, the names of the ships and the dates of passage are given.

per hundred pounds; he had to furnish the immigrants on their arrival and for the first year, with provisions and with agricultural implements, seeds and animals.

The only advantages that Castro derived was the right of retaining one-half of the land assigned to each settler of his colonies. By the law of 1850, entitled, "An Act to Perfect Land Titles in Castro's Colony," which was approved January 22, 1860, the certificates were issued directly to the colonists, and Castro lost his land and received nothing for the services he had rendered to Texas, and for colonizing the territory west of San Antonio.

Most of the colonists came from the French Departments of High and Low Rhin, Meurthe, Moselle, Doubs and Jura; or from Alsace and Lorraine and Franche Comté.[17]

During the Civil War these settlements remained loyal to the Union. A majority of the population was Catholic.

THE COMMUNISTIC COLONY OF BETTINA.

In 1846, a colony was organized in Darmstadt, which was socialistic in its tendencies. It received its name from Bettina von Arnim, the German writer and friend of Goethe. The leaders of the plan to form a communistic settlement were Spies, the successor of Meusebach as Commissioner General of the Mainzerverein, and Dr. Ferdinand Herff. On his return to Germany, Solms Braunfels delivered many speeches. These, together with his writings, as well as those of Spies, had a great influence over the students of Giessen and Heidelberg. One of the future members of the colony heard Solms speak and declares that the latter described Texas as a "land of milk and honey, of perennial flowers, of crystal streams rich and fruitful beyond measure, where roamed myriads of deer and buffalo, while the primeval forests abounded in wild fowl of every kind.[18] Solms further declared in a speech delivered to a school in Darmstadt, that there was no demand in the Old Country for all

---

[17] Castro, Henri, *Le Texas Anvers*, 1845, gives Castro's own account of the settlements.
[18] *Texas Historical Quarterly*, Vol. III, p. 34.

the professional men whom the universities were turning out, and that they must find a new and developing country where their services would be in demand.

Gustav Schleicher, at that time a civil engineer, became one of the members of the colony. There were some forty young men who participated in its organization. Its watchwords were friendship, freedom and equality. The majority of those taking part in the enterprise was composed of educated young men. There were in the undertaking two physicians, one engineer, one architect, seven lawyers, four foresters, one student of theology and a lieutenant of artillery. The rest were mainly farmers and mechanics.

The first colonists landed in New York in 1846; from there they went via railroad to Wheeling (West Virginia); from there, via stage to New Orleans and thence via water to Galveston. They landed at Indianola in 1847 and reached New Braunfels in August of that year. Meusebach had already made his treaty with the Indians and the new colony was established in the Fischer and Miller grant west of Fredericksburg. The members engaged in stock raising and agriculture, and the venture, on account of its lack of government, and because of Mexican and Indian depredations, became a failure.[19]

GERMAN-SWISS COLONIES IN TEXAS.

German-Swiss colonies are found in the cities of Dallas, San Antonio, Galveston and Houston. The first German-Swiss to settle in any numbers came to Texas in 1855, and became members of Victor Considerant's Communistic Colony, near Dallas, Texas, which was founded in Paris in 1852. This colony was given up on account of its debts. In 1868 and in 1872, two colonies of Swiss were settled near Dallas. In 1880, there were two hundred Swiss in that city. They had a Gesangverein, a Turnverein and during that year held a "Mai-Fest." In 1888,

---

[19] This account is based on an article, The Communistic Colony of Bettina, in Vol. III, p. 33ff, in the *Texas Hist. Ass'n Quarterly;* on *Memorial Addresses;* and on account by Doctor Herff in *Collier, Hist. of San Antonio;* and on an article in *Allgemeine Zeitung*, March 3, 1847, No. 62.

there was a colony of 160 Swiss in Houston. It also had its special societies. Capitalists of Basel founded a colony of Swiss on the Guadaloupe river. The colony of New Baden, Texas, contained several German-Swiss. Mrs. Louisa Storer, formerly the wife of Friedrich Ernst, one of the first Germans to settle in Texas, was a Swiss.[20]

BIBLIOGRAPHY.

WORKS CONTAINING BIBLIOGRAPHICAL REFERENCES.

Baker, T. S.: Lenau and Young Germany in America, Philadelphia, 1897.
Bruncken, Ernest: The Germans in America, American Historical Association Report, 1898, pp. 347 to 354, Washington, 1899.
Faust, Albert B.: The German Element in the United States, Boston, 1909.
Griffin, A. P. C.: A List of Works Relating to the Germans in the United States, Washington, 1904.
Raines, C. W.: Bibliography of Texas, Austin, 1896.
Slauson, Alan B.: A Check List of American Newspapers in the Library of Congress, Washington, 1901.
Sabin, Joseph: A Dictionary of Books Relating to America from its Discovery to the Present Time, New York, 1868 to 1892.

PERIODICALS AND NEWSPAPERS.

Allgemeine Auswanderungs Zeitung, Rudolstadt, 1846.
Allgemeine Zeitung, Mar. 3, 1847.
Americana Germanica, Editor, M. D. Learned, New York and London, 1897 to 1902 (Continued as German American Annals).
Atlantische Studien von Deutschen in Amerika, Vols. I to VIII, Goettingen, 1853 to 1857.
Bibliothéque Universelle de Genève, Vol. 35, 1857, p. 297; N. P. Vol. 63, 1878, p. 128.
Civilian and Galveston Gazette, January 7, 1843, and Dec. 2, 1843.
Deutsche Pionier der, Erinnerungen aus dem Pionier-Leben der Deutschen in Amerika, Vols. 1 to 18, Cincinnati, Ohio, 1869 to 1885.
Deutsch-Amerikanische Geschichtsblätter, 1901 to 1906, Chicago, Ill.

---

[20] This is based on Steinach, Alderich, Dr., *Geschichte und Leben der schweizer Kolonien in den Vereinigten Staaten von Nord Amerika*, New York, 1889.

Deutsch-Amerikanisches Magazin, Cincinnati, 1886 to 1887.
Galveston Weekly News, March 20, 1847.
Houston Post, September 14, 1842.
Houston Telegraph, Dec. 11, 1839; Feb. 1, 1843; May 10, 1847; June 7, 1847; June 14, 1847; June 19, 1847; Oct. 24, 1847; Mar. 30, 1848; Dec. 7, 1848; Oct. 30, 1850; Dec. 6, 1850; June 14, 1857.
Magazin für die Literatur des Auslandes, Leipzig, 1847.
Mercantile Advertiser, Houston, Dec. 8 and 15, 1849.
New Braunfels Zeitung, May 27, 1870.
New York Independent, Oct. 22, 1857.
New York Daily Tribune, Jan. 20, 1855; June 13, 1857.
New York Weekly Tribune, May 9, 1857.
Niles Weekly Register, Vol. 43 or Vol. VII, Fourth Series, 1832, 1833.
San Antonio Express, Oct. 4 and 5, 1903.
San Antonio Ledger, May 18, 1854; July 20, 1854; Oct. 1, 1855; July 25, 1857; Sept. 26, 1857; Dec. 26, 1857; Jan. 26, 1858; Feb. 27, 1858; Sept. 27, 1858.
Schuetze, Albert, editor, Jahrbuch für Texas und Emigranten Führer, Austin, 1882 to 1884.
Schuetze's Monatsbuch für Texas, Austin, 1904.
Southern Intelligencer, Austin, May 27, 1857; June 3, 1857; May 15, 1858; Dec. 22, 1858; Apr. 6, 1859; June 8, 1859.
Tait's Edinburgh Magazine, n. s., Vol. 15, 1848.
Texas Almanac, 1857 to 1861 (inclusive); 1867 to 1873 (inclusive), Galveston.
Texas State Gazette, Austin, June 22, 1854; July 8, 1854; July 22, 1854; July 29, 1854; June 16, 1855; July 11, 1855; July 25, 1855; Sept. 16, 1855; Sept. 22, 1855; Sept. 29, 1855; Oct. 6, 1855; Oct. 20, 1855; Dec. 29, 1855; May 16, 1856; May 24, 1856; Sept. 6, 1856; Sept. 27, 1856; Nov. 15, 1856; July 11, 1857; July 29, 1857; May 15, 1858; Dec. 16, 1858; Dec. 22, 1858; Dec. 25, 1858; Mar. 24, 1860; Aug. 25, 1860; Dec. 15, 1860.
Texas Historical Association Quarterly, Vols. I, II and III, Austin, Texas, 1897 to 1900.
The Passing Show, San Antonio, Feb. 23, 1907.
Turn Zeitung, Organ des Socialistischen Turnerbundes, New York, Sept. 5, 1853.
Victoria (Texas) Advocate, Feb. 10, 1847.

BOOKS.

Achenbach, Hermann: Tagebuch meiner Reise in den nordamerikanischen Freistaaten, Düsseldorf, 1835.

Aufforderung und Erklärung in Betreff einer Auswanderung im Grossen aus Deutschland in die nordamerikanischen Freistaaten, Giessen, 1833.
Auswanderer nach Texas der. Ein Handbuch und Rathgeber für die, welche sich in Texas ansiedeln wollen. Bremen, 1846.
Baker, Thomas Stockham: Lenau and Young Germany in America, Philadelphia, 1897.
Behr von, Ottomar: Guter Rath für Auswanderer nach den Vereinigten Staaten von Nord Amerika mit besonderer Berücksichtigung von Texas, Leipzig, 1847.
Berghaus, Heinrich: Die Vereinigten Staaten von Nord Amerika, Gotha, 1848.
Beyer, Moritz: Das Auswanderungsbuch oder Führer und Rathgeber bei der Auswanderung nach Nord Amerika und Texas, Leipzig, 1846.
Bracht, Viktor: Texas im Jahre 1848, Elberfeld und Iserlohn, 1849.
Bromme, Traugott: Neustes vollständigstes Hand- und Reisebuch für Auswanderer, Bayreuth, 1846.
Bromme, Traugott: Neustes vollständigstes Hand- und Reisebuch für Auswanderer nach den Vereinigten Staaten von Nord Amerika, Siebente vermehrte und verbesserte Auflage von Buettner, Bamberg, 1853.
Brown, John Henry: Indian Wars and Pioneers of Texas; Austin.
Bruncken, Ernest: German Political Refugees in America, 1815 to 1860; Chicago, 1904 (reprint of Deutsch-Amerikanische-Geschichtsblätter, 1904).
Busey, Samuel C., M. D.: Immigration, Its Evils and Consequences; New York, 1856.
Buettner, J. G.: Briefe aus und über Amerika, oder Beiträge zu einer richtigen Kenntniss der Vereinigten Staaten von Nord Amerika und ihrer Bewohner; Dresden and Leipzig, 1845.
Castro, Henri: Le Texas; Anvers, 1845.
Castro, Lorenzo: Immigration from Alsace and Lorraine. A Brief Sketch of the History of Castro's Colony in Western Texas; New York, 1871.
Census of United States, 1850, 1860, 1870, 1900.
Corner, William: San Antonio de Bexar; San Antonio, 1890.
Dallam's Texas Law Reports, Vol. XXX.
Deiler, J. Hanno: Geschichte der deutschen Gesellschaft von New Orleans; New Orleans, 1897.
Deutschen Ansiedelungen in Texas, die. Bonn, 1845.
Douai, Adolf: Land und Leute in Amerika; Berlin, 1864.
Duden, Gottfried: Bericht über eine Reise nach den westlichen Staaten Nordamerikas und eine mehrjährigen Aufenthalt am Missouri in den Jahren, 1824, 1825, 1826, 1827. St. Gallen, 1832.

Ehrenberg, Hermann: Der Freiheitskampf in Texas; Leipzig, 1844.
Ehrenberg, Hermann: Fahrten und Schicksale eines Deutschen in Texas; Leipzig, 1845.
Ehrenberg, Hermann: Texas und seine Revolution; Leipzig, 1843.
Eichhoff, Anton: In der neuen Heimath (zweite Ausgabe). New York, 1885.
Enzlberger, Johannes: Schematismus; Katholische Geistlichkeit der deutschen Zunge in den Vereinigten Staaten; Milwaukee, 1892.
Faust, Albert B.: Charles Sealsfield (Carl Postl) Materials for a Biography, a Study of his Style; His Influence upon American Literature; Baltimore, 1892.
Faust, Albert B.: The German Element in the United States, Boston, 1909.
Faust, Albert B.: Charles Sealsfield (Carl Postl), der Dichter beider Hemisphären, Weimar, 1897.
Fest-Ausgabe zum fünfzigjährigen Jubiläum der deutschen Kolonie Friedrichsburg. Eine kurzgefasste Entwickelungs-Geschichte der vom Mainzer Adelsverein gegründeten Kolonien in Texas. Fredericksburg, Texas, 1896.
Fleischmann, C. L.: Wegweiser und Rathgeber nach und in den Vereinigten Staaten von Nord Amerika. Stuttgart, 1852.
Froebel, Julius: Seven Years Travel in Central America, Northern Mexico and the Far West of the United States. London, 1859.
Gammel, H. P. N.: Laws of Texas, Vol. II. 11 Vols. Austin, 1902.
Goegg, Amand: Ueberseeische Reisen; Zürich, 1888.
Goldbeck, Fritz: Seit fünfzig Jahren. Prosa in Versen; Skizzen aus Zeit der ersten deutschen Einwanderung in West Texas, 1844, 1845, 1846. San Antonio, 1895.
Gottschall, Rudolf: Die deutsche National Literatur in der ersten Hälfte des neunzehnten Jahrhunderts; Breslau, 1861.
Gonnard, René: L'Émigration europeéne au XIXe Siécle; Paris, 1906.
Grund, Francis J.: Handbuch und Wegweiser für Auswanderer nach den Vereinigten Staaten von Nord Amerika und Texas; Stuttgart and Tubingen, 1846.
Grund, F. J.: The Americans. 2 Vols. London, 1837.
Guide to Western Texas, 1876.
Halle, Ernst von: Baumwoll Produktion und Pflanzungswirtschaft in den nordamerikanischen Südstaaten (Staat und Socialwissenschaftliche Forschungen. Band XV: Heft I).
Hammond, M. B.: The Cotton Industry: An Essay in American Economic History. Publications American Economic Association, n. s. No. 1 (Dec. 1897). New York, 1897.
Handbuch des Deutschthums im Auslande; Berlin, 1904.

Harkort, Eduard: Aus mijicanischen Gefängnissen, Buchstück aus E. H's hinterlassenen Papieren. Herausgegeben von Dr. F. G. Kühne. Leipzig, 1858.
Hartley: Digest of Laws of Texas; Austin, 1850.
Hecke, J. Valentin: Reise durch die Vereinigten Staaten von Nord Amerika in den Jahren 1818-1819; two Vols., Berlin, 1821.
Helper, Hinton H.: The Impending Crisis of the South; New York, 1860.
Hillquit, Morris: History of Socialism in the United States; New York and London, 1903.
Hoehne, Friedrich: Wahn und Ueberzeugung. Seine Reise in Weimar über Bremen nach Nordamerika und Texas in den Jahren 1839-1841; Weimar 1844.
Holst, Hermann: Eduard von: Constitutional and Political History of the United States, Translated by John J. Lalor et al.; 8 Vols., Chicago, 1877 to 1892.
Kapp, Friedrich: Aus und über Amerika, Thatsachen und Erlebnisse, 2 Vols., Berlin, 1876.
Kapp, Friederich: Die Geschichte der deutschen Ansiedelungen des westlichen Texas und dessen Bedeutung für die Vereinigten Staaten (in Atlantische Studien, Vol. I, p. 173 ff).
Kapp, Friederich: The History of Texas, Early German Colonization, Princes and Nobles in America, the Future of the State; (in New York Tribune, Jan. 20, 1855).
Kennedy, William: Geographie, Natur-Geschichte und Topographie von Texas, Translated by Otto von Czarnowsky, Frankfurt a. M., 1846.
Kennedy, William: Texas, Its History, Geography, Natural History and Topography; London, 1840. 2 Vols.
King, Edward: Southern States of North America. A Record of Journeys in Texas; 4 Vols., London, 1875.
Koerner, Gustav: Das deutsche Element in den Vereinigten Staaten von Nord Amerika, 1818-1848; Cincinnati, 1880.
Kordül, A.: Führer nach und in Texas; Rottweil am Neckar, 1846.
Loeher, Franz: Geschichte und Zustände der Deutschen in Amerika; Cincinnati und Leipzig, 1847.
Lohmann, F. H..: Comfort, Fest-Schrift zur fünfzig-jährigen Jubelfeier der Ansiedlung. Comfort, Texas, 1904.
Martin, Ludwig: Der nordamerikanische Freistaat Texas; Wiesbaden, 1848.
Matthes, Benno: Reise-bilder. Bilder aus Texas; Dresden, 1861.
Menzel, Gottfried: Die Vereinigten Staaten von Nord-Amerika; Berlin, 1853.
Meusebach, John O.: Answers to Interrogatories; Austin, 1894.
Mgebroff, Johannes: Geschichte der ersten deutschen evangelischen-lutherischen Synode in Texas; Austin, 1902.

Nachrichten für Auswanderer; Eisleben, 1846.
Neuste Briefe und Nachrichten aus Texas; Heilbron, 1846.
Nies, Conrad: Aus westlichen Weiten; Leipzig, 1905.
Olmsted, Frederick Law: A Journey through Texas or a Saddle Trip on the Southwestern Frontier (Our Slave States, Vol. II) New York, 1860.
Olmsted, Frederick Law: The Cotton Kingdom: A Traveller's Observations on Cotton and Slavery in the American Slave States; 2 Vols. New York, 1862.
Rather, Ethel Zither: De Witt's Colony; Texas Historical Association Quarterly, 1904-5.
Roemer, Ferdinand: Texas. Mit besonderer Rücksicht auf deutsche Auswanderung und die physischen Verhältnisse des Landes; Bonn, 1849.
Rosenberg, William von: Kritik der Geschichte des Vereins zum Schutze der deutschen Auswanderer nach Texas; Austin, 1894.
Ross, George M. von: Der nordamerikanische Freistaat Texas nach eigener Anschauung und nach den neuesten und besten Quellen für deutsche Auswanderer. Rudolstadt, 1851.
Schem, Alexander T.: Deutsch-Amerikanisches Konversations-Lexicon; Vol. X, New York, 1873.
Scherpf, G. A.: Entstehungsgeschichte und gegenwärtiger Zustand des neuen unabhängigen amerikanischen Staats Texas. Ein Beitrag zur Geschichte, Statistik und Geographie dieses Jahrhunderts, im Lande selbst gesammelt. Augsburg, 1841.
Schleicher, Gustave: Memorial Addresses on the Life and Character of Gustave Schleicher. (Published by order of Congress), Washington, 1880.
Schmidt, Karl: Dies Buch gehört den deutschen Auswanderer; Leipzig, 1853.
Sealsfield, Charles (Carl Postl): Das Cajütenbuch oder nationale Characteristiken; 2 Vols. Zürich, 1841.
Sealsfield, Charles: Life in the New World or Sketches of American Society. Translated from the German by G. C. Mackay; New York, 1844.
Sealsfield, Charles: Nathan, der Squatter oder der erste Amerikaner in Texas; Zürich, 1837.
Sealsfield, Charles: The Cabin Book or Sketches of Life in Texas. Translated from the German by C. H. Mersch. New York, 1844.
Seele, Hermann: A Short History of Comal County, Texas. New Braunfels, 1885.
Seele, Hermann: Die deutsche Colonie New Braunfels, Jahrbuch für Texas, 1884.
Senate Documents, 38th Congress, First Session, Doc. 341.
Siemering, A.: Ein verfehltes Leben; Eine Novelle. San Antonio, 1876.

Smith, Edward, M. D.: Account of a Journey through North-Eastern Texas; London, 1849.
Soergel, Alwin H.: Für Auswanderungslustige! Briefe eines unter dem Schutze des Mainzer Vereins nach Texas Ausgewanderten. Leipzig, 1847.
Soergel, Alwin H.: Neuste Nachrichten aus Texas; Eisleben, 1847.
Solms-Braunfels, Carl, Prinz zu: Texas; Geschildert in Beziehung auf seine geographischen, socialen und übrigen Verhältnisse, mit besonderer Rücksicht auf die deutsche Colonisation. Ein Handbuch für Auswanderer nach Texas. Frankfurt am Main, 1846.
Sommer, Karl von: Bericht über meine Reise nach Texas im Jahre 1846. Bremen 1847.
Steinach, Alderich, Dr.: Geschichte und Leben der schweizer Kolonien in den Vereinigten Staaten von Nord Amerika; New York, 1889.
Tenner, Armin: Amerika, Der heutige Standpunk der Kultur in den Vereinigten Staaten. Berlin, 1886.
Texas, Ein Handbuch für deutsche Auswanderer mit besonderer Rücksicht auf diejenigen, welche ihre Ueberfahrt und Ansiedelung durch Hilfe des Vereins zum Schutze deutscher Einwanderer in Texas bewirken sollen. (Official publication of the Verein), Bremen, 1846.
United States Statutes at Large, Vol. IX.
Wappäus, J. E.: Deutsche Auswanderung und Colonisation; Leipzig, 1846-1848.
Wooten, Dudley G.: A Comprehensive History of Texas. 1685 to 1897. 2 Vols. Dallas, 1898.
Wrede, Friederich von: Lebensbilder aus den Vereinigten Staaten von Nord Amerika und Texas. Cassel, 1844.

APPENDIX A.

(Germans in the Texan War for Independence. Rosenberg, Kritik p. 7.)

The following Germans are named in the archives of Texas among those who took part in the Revolution of 1836:—
Carl Amsler, Louis L. Amelung, Jacob Albrecht, Wm. Ahlert, Joseph Biegel, Joh. Brugiesky, Joh. A. Baumacher, Thomas Bertram, W. M. Burch, Franz Dieterich, N. Dombriski, George B. Erath, F. G. Elm, Herman Ehrenberg, Conrad Eigenauer, Bernhard Eilers, Fritz Ernst, Algert Emanuel, Joseph Ellinger, Carl Fordtran, Carl A. Felder, Abraham Formann, Peter H. Fullenweider, Wilhelm

Frels, Wilhelm Friedländer, F. W. Grasmeyer, Jacob H. Geiger, Friederich Griebenrath, Conrad Gürgens, Carl Giesecke, Joseph Herz, Christian Hillebrandt, Moriz Heinrich, Georg Herder, Joh. F. Hollien, Joh. Heunecke, Eduart Harkort, J. A. Heiser, F. W. Heuseman, Herman Halt, Caspar Harnmacher, Friedrich Helmüller, Louis Kleberg, Robert Kleberg, August Kinchel, Louis Knup, Joh. Köpf, A. D. Kessler, Franz Keller, Louis Kratz, Anton Lehmkuhl, Georg W. Lückenhoger, Carl Lyninburg, Wilhelm Langenheim, G. W. Lück, Friederich Lundt, Ferdinand Lüders, Carl Messer, Friederich Niebling, Johann Oberländer, Joh. Peske, Peter Pieper, W. G. Preusch, J. P. Reinhardt, Eugen Pucholasky, August Carl Redlich, Geo. W. Ricks, W. Rosenberg, L. S. von Röder, Albrecht v. Röder, Joachim v. Röder, Louis v. Röder, Otto v. Röder, Rudolph v. Röder, Wilhelm v. Röder, Louis Schulz, H. Schulz, J. Schür, Adolph Stern, R. Stölke, Friederich Schrack, C. U. Schütz, Ferdinand Schröder, Georg Sullsbach, Henry Thürwächter, Carl Tapps, J. Q. Volckmar, Samuel Wolfenberger, Wm. Wagner, Henry Wilke, Philip Weppler, Jacob Wilhelm, Richard Wilhelm, Louis v. Zacharius, Joh. Zekainsky.

APPENDIX B.

Texas.

Ein Handbuch für deutsche Auswanderer. Bremen, 1846, pp. 63 ff.

Ueber den Verein zum Schutze deutscher Einwanderer in Texas.

Im Frühling des Jahres 1844 brachten die öffentlichen Blätter nachfolgende Bekanntmachung:

Ein Verein hat sich gebildet, dessen Zweck es ist, die deutsche Auswanderung so viel als möglich nach einem einzigen, günstig gelegenen Punkte hinzuleiten, die Auswanderer auf der weiten Reise und in der neuen Heimath zu unterstützen und nach Kräften dahin zu wirken, dass ihnen jenseits des Meeres eine neue Heimath gesichert werde.

Der Verein erlässt diese Bekanntmachung nicht in der Absicht, Geldkräfte für sein Unternehmen zu gewinnen; das Geschäfts-Kapital ist bereits vollständig gezeichnet. Allein im Bewusstsein des guten Zweckes ist er es dem Publikum und sich selbst schuldig, die Gründe, welche den Verein in's Leben gerufen, die Art und Weise, wie er seine Aufgabe zu lösen hofft, und die Grundsätze, die ihn dabei leiten, offen darzulegen.

Der Verein will den Trieb zur Auswanderung weder anregen, noch entschuldigen. Genug, das Bedürfniss besteht einmal, und lässt sich leider eben so wenig wegläugnen, als es möglich ist, jenem immer lebendigeren Triebe Einhalt zu thun. Vielfältige Ursachen wirken dabei zusammen; die Verdrängung der Handarbeit durch das Maschinenwesen, die grossen, fast periodischen Unfälle, die den Handel heimsuchen, die zunehmende Verarmung, eine Folge der Uebervölkerung und des Mangels an Arbeit; endlich wohl auch der gerühmte Reichthum des Bodens im neuen Lande und die manchmal belohnte, oft getäuschte Hoffnung auf ein besseres Seyn und Wirken jenseits der Meere.

Unter solchen Verhältnissen mussten die Auswanderer in der That einem besseren Loose entgegen gehen, wenn sie, in wohlgeordneter Masse zusammenhaltend, eine richtige Leitung und einen wirksamen Schutz in der Fremde fänden. Und somit ist die Nothwendigkeit wie der Zweck des Vereins von selbst gegeben: er will es versuchen, die Auswanderung zu regeln, und zu leiten, damit die Möglichkeit gegeben werde, dass die Deutschen in Amerika eine deutsche Heimath wiederfinden, und aus dem ununterbrochenen Zusammehange unter sich und mit dem alten Vaterlande ein gewerblicher und Handelsverkehr entstehe, der beiden zum materiellen und geistigen Gewinn gereichen muss. Auf diese Weise wünscht der Verein das Seinige zu thun zu Deutschlands Ehre und Wohl beizutragen, um vielleicht den deutschen Armen eine belohnende Thätigkeit, dem deutschen Gewerbfleiss neue Märkte, dem deutschen Seehandel eine weitere Ausdehnung dereinst zu eröffnen.

Nach langer, sorgfältiger Prüfung hat sich der Verein dafür entschieden, dass Texas dasjenige Land ist, welches dem deutschen Auswanderer am besten zusagen möchte. Das gesunde Clima, die Fruchtbarkeit des Bodens, der Reichthum seiner Erzeugnisse und die Leichtigkeit der Verbindungen mit Europa haben schon seit längerer Zeit eine grosse Zahl von auswanderungslustigen Deutschen dahin gezogen, die jedoch, ohne Schutz und Schirm, sich vereinzelten, und leider oft ganz zu Grunde gingen. Um so mehr musste sich die Aufmerksamkeit des Vereins nach diesen Gegenden wenden. Durch erfahrene und des Landes kundige Männer hat er das texanische Gebiet bereisen lassen, und so vollständige Aufschlüsse erhalten, dass er mit gutem Gewissen und voller Ueberzeugung seine Wahl treffen konnte.

Der Verein hat im gesundesten Theile jenes Landes ein zusammenhängendes noch unbebautes Gebiet von beträchtlichem Umfang erworben, wird dort die Ansiedlung derjenigen Deutschen die das alte Vaterland verlassen, nach Kräften befördern, und hierzu die von den Verhältnissen gebotenen, zweckdienstlichsten Mittel anwenden.

Vor dem Abgang wird jedem Auswanderer eine Strecke gutes Landes schriftlich zugesichert, welches er bei seiner Ankunft als Geschenk, ohne alle jetzige oder künftige Vergütung, vom Vereine erhält. Dieser Boden, dessen grösserer oder geringerer Flächenraum sich nach der Grösse der Familie richtet, wird freies Eigenthum des Auswanderers, sobald er drei Jahre lang auf seinem Gute gewohnt. Aber auch vor Ablauf dieser drei Jahre gehören ihm die

Erzeugnisse seines Bodens, und der Verein macht weder auf jene, noch auf diesen den geringsten Anspruch.

Der Verein ist ferner dafür bemüht, gute und geräumige Schiffe für die Ueberfahrt auszuwählen; er sorgt dafür, dass es an gesunder, wohlfeiler Nahrung nicht fehle, und die Reisekosten so gering als möglich ausfallen. An den Landungsplätzen sind besondere Agenten damit beauftragt, den Auswanderern mit Rath und That an die Hand zu gehen; die Letzeren finden hier Wagen bereit, die sie mit ihrer Habe unentgeldlich an den Ort ihrer Ansiedlung führen. Auch für ihre Bedürfnisse unterweges wird Vorsorge getroffen. So wie sie an Ort und Stelle anlangen, wird jeder Familie ein eigenes Haus eingeräumt, versteht sich, nur nach dortiger Art aus aufeinander gelegten Balken gezimmert; Vorrathshäuser mit Lebensmitteln, Werkzeugen für Garten und Ackerbau, Samen und Pflanzen aller Art wohl versehen, sichern ihnen Alles, was sie zur Arbeit und zum Leben bedürfen; ebenso finden sie die nöthigen Hausthiere, als Pflugochsen, Pferde, Kühe, Schweine, Schafe, schon an Ort und Stelle. Alles dies wird ihnen zu einem viel geringeren Preise verkauft, als die nämlichen Gegenstände auf den nächstgelegenen Märkten zu haben sind. Solche Auswanderer, deren Betragen und Thätigkeit sich besonders bewährt, erhalten von Seiten der Verwaltung Vorschüsse, die von der ersten Ernte zurückzuzahlen sind.

Den Auswanderern steht es frei, die Erzeugnisse ihres Ackerbaues und ihrer Gewerbsthätigkeit an die Magazine des Vereins zu veräussern.

Für sittliche und religiöse Erziehung der Kinder zu sorgen, betrachtet der Verein als eine heilige Pflicht; er wird daher, je nach den Bedürfnissen der Bevölkerung, Kirchen und Schulen in der Kolonie errichten lassen. Er wird nicht minder für die Anstellung von Aerzten und Apothekern, so wie für Gründung eines Krankenhauses Sorge tragen.

Eine Gemeindeverfassung und eine Gerichtsordnung, beide nach dem Vorbilde der in Texas anerkannten englischen, werden, sobald es nur thunlich, durch die Verwaltung der Ansiedlungen hergestellt.

Sollten sich unter den Auswandereren einzelne zur Rückkehr nach Europa bewogen finden, so wird ihnen die Heimfahrt zu den nämlichen Preisen, wie die Hinfahrt, auf den Schiffen des Vereins zugesichert.

Der erste Zug von Auswanderern geht im September dieses Jahres 1844 ab; allein schon im Mai werden zwei Mitglieder des Vereins nach Texas reisen, um dort Vorbereitungen zur Aufnahme der Auswanderer zu treffen und die Verwaltung der Ansiedelungen vorläufig einzurichten.

Der Verein wird drei Prozent seiner Einnahme dazu verwenden, um dürftigen Auswanderern die Ueberfahrt und Ansiedelung zu erleichtern. Vorläufig jedoch und bis er diese Absicht zu wirklichen im Stande ist, kann die Niederlassung in der Kolonie nur Denjenigen zugestanden werden, welche die unumgänglich erförderlichen Geldmittel besitzen.

Der unverheirathete Einwanderer bedarf wenigstens ein Capital von 300 Gulden.

Das Haupt einer nicht zahlreichen Familie ein Capital von 600 Gulden.

Um aber auch einer wenn gleich nur kleinen Anzahl von ärmeren Familien sogleich die Ansiedelung möglich zu machen, wird der Verein—in dem er glaubt, den edlen Gesinnungen, die man ihm bereits zu erkennen gegeben, dadurch am besten entgegen zu kommen—eine Liste zu freiwilliger Unterzeichnung eröffnen, deren Ertrag ausscliesslich zu diesem Zwecke bestimmt ist. Jährlich sollen sodann die Beiträge und deren Verwendung, so wie die Namen der Wohlthäter in den gelesensten Blättern Deutschlands bekannt gemacht werden.

Wenn der Verein auf diese Weise, so viel in seinen Kräften steht, dem Unternehmen einen glücklichen Erfolg zu sichern bemüht ist, so beruht doch das Gelingen am meisten auf der ernsten unverdrossenen Thätigkeit der Auswanderer selbst. Das neue Vaterland jenseits des Oceans wird nur dann gedeihlich emporblühen, wenn die Deutschen auch dort sich bewähren, wie sie stets in der Heimath waren: arbeitsam, beharrlich, treu der guten Sitte und dem Gesetze. Darf der Verein auch hieran nicht zweifeln, so wird er doch, um nicht das Wohl und Wehe deutscher Landsleute den Zufälligkeiten eines Versuches preiszugeben, im Laufe dieses Jahres fürs erste nur ein Hundert und fünfzig Familien zur Uebersiedelung zulassen, und erst dann, wenn diese eine wohlgesicherte Niederlassung gegründet haben, einer weiteren Auswanderung mit Rath und That anhanden gehen.

Genauere Aufschlüsse und Auskunft jeder Art werden auf frankirte briefliche Anfragen ertheilt:

Zu Mainz bei der Verwaltung des Vereins zum Schutze deutscher Einwanderer in Texas.

Zu Frankfurt a. M. bei Hrn. *L. H. Flersheim*, Banquier des Vereins.

Gefertigt durch den leitenden Ausschuss des Vereins.

Mainz, den 9. April 1844.

(gez.) *Fürst zu Leiningen.*

In Verhinderung des Grafen Carl zu Castell:

Graf zu Isenburg-Meerholz.

APPENDIX C.

Organische Statute der Colonization.*

I. Bedingungen der Annahme.

Art. 1. Um als Mitglied der Colonie aufgenommen zu werden, bedürfen die Einwanderer folgende Urkunden:
1. Einen Geburts-akt.
2. Einen Copulations-Schein, wenn sie verheirathet sind.
3. Ein Moralitäts-Zeugniss ihrer früheren Ortsbehörde.

Art. 2. Bis andere Bestimmungen erfolgen, haben dieselben genügende Mittel nachzuweisen um sowohl die Kosten der Ueberfahrt, als jene des Unterhaltes in der Colonie während der ersten 6 Monate zu decken.

Art. 3. Dieselben haben sich 3 Tage vor der Abreise an dem Einschiffungsorte einzufinden. Nur vermittelst eines Annahme-Zeugnisses ausgestellt von der Administration, werden sie auf den Fahrzeugen des Vereins zugelassen.

Art. 4. Die Kosten der Ueberfahrt zerfallen in 2 Classen: *Ueberfahrt mit Verköstigung, Ueberfahrt ohne Verköstigung.* Auswanderer, welche der letzten Classe sich anschliessen, haben zureichenden Vorrath für einen Zeitraum von 2 Monaten—muthmassliche Dauer der Ueberfahrt—nachzuweisen.

Verbindlichkeiten des Vereins.

Art. 5. Der Verein giebt jedem Familienhaupte, welches nach dessen Colonie in Texas sich begiebt, von seinem Besitzungen 320 Acres Landes, amerikanisches Maas, ungefähr 500 Morgen deutsche Mässung. Jeder unverheirathete Einwanderer, der wenigstens 17 Jahre zählt, hat Ansprüche auf die Hälfte dieses Quantums.

    Im Augenblick der Abreise wird jedem Einwanderer ein provisorischer Erwerbstitel zugestellt, welcher später —nach Ausweis des Art. 23—gegen einen definitiven Erwerbstitel ungetauscht wird.

Art. 6. Es enthält dieser provisorische Erwerbstitel die Ordnungs-Nummer, welche das Loos bezeichnet, auf welches dem Einwanderer Eigenthums-Ansprüche zustehen. Die Einweisung in das bewilligte Grundeigenthum geschieht an Ort und Stelle.

Art. 7. Es stellt der Verein unentgeltlich die Transport-Mittel für Familie und Geräthschaften der Einwanderer vom Anlandungsorte nach der Colonie.

    Die Fürsorge des Vereins wird—sollte sie es sachdienlich erachten—einen Dampfbootdienst auf den Flüssen herstellen.

---

* *Handbuch*, pp. 90-96.

Art. 8. Es sorgt der Verein für Nahrung und Unterkunft der Einwanderer vom Landungspunkte bis zur Ankunft in der Colonie. Für letzere findet keine Rückvergütigung statt, wohl aber für erstere.

Art. 9. Um der Einwanderer Existenz zu erleichtern und denselben die Mittel zur Arbeit zu verschaffen, wird der Verein in der Colonie selbst ein Magazin—einen Bazar—eröffnen, welches alle nöthigen Lebensbedürfnisse, alle Acker- und Handwerksgeräthe, die Sämereien und überhaupt alle einer Colonie unentbehrlichen Gegenstände darbietet.
Es sorgt der Verein für das zum Ackerbau nöthige Zugvieh.
Alle diese Gegenstände sowohl als das Zugvieh werden dem Einwanderer zu dem Preise geliefert, wie solcher sich in der der Colonie zunächst belegenen Stadt herausstellt.

Art. 10. Natural-Vorschüsse werden denjenigen Einwanderern gewährt werden, welche sich durch Aufführung und Thätigkeit zur Arbeit bei der Colonial-Direction empfohlen haben.
Als Garantie für Rückzahlung dieser gemachten Vorschüsse haften die Besitzungen der Colonisten.

Art. 11. Um das Unterbringen der Ackerbau- und industriellen Ereignisse der Colonie zu erleichtern, wird das Comptoir des Vereins diese Produkte für eigene Rechnung und nach dem kostenden Preise kaufen oder Sorge tragen, sie für Rechnung der Colonisten am Orte selbst oder auswärts gegen eine einfache Commissions-Gebühr von 5 Proc.—die üblichen Umschlags-Kosten nicht eingerechnet—zu verkaufen. Jedenfalls steht es den Colonisten indessen frei, ihre Produkte direkt und nach Gutdünken zu verkaufen.

Art. 12. Bis die Bevölkerung zu der Seelenzahl gediehen ist, um selbst die Kosten eines Gottesdienstes zu bestreiten, stellt ihr der Verein eine Kirche zur Verfügung, in welcher die Religions-Uebungen der verschiedenen Culten, zu denen die Colonisten zählen, gefeiert werden können.
Eine besondere Anordnung wird die Stunden für Abhaltungen dieser Uebungen normiren.

Art. 13. Es wird eine Primär-Schule für die Kinder der Einwanderer ins Leben gerufen. Sie empfangen darin:
 1. Religions-Unterricht,
 2. Unterricht im Lesen,
 3. Unterricht im Schreiben,
 4. Rechnen-Unterricht und endlich,
 5. Unterricht in der deutschen und englischen Sprache.

Art. 14. Es wird in der Colonie eine ärztliche Hülfs-Anstalt, eine Apotheke und ein Reconvalescenten-Haus errichtet werden.

Art. 15. Es stiftet der Verein eine Spar-Casse in welche die Colonisten ihre Ersparnisse niederlegen können. Sie gewährt 5 Proc. Zinsen.

    Auf Vorschlag der Colonial-Direction wird der Verein die Art der Einlegung und Zurückziehung der Einlage-Quoten, das Maximum der einzulegenden Beträge normiren.

Art. 16. Unmittelbar nach Ankunft der ersten Einwanderer wird eine Munizipal-Einrichtung geschaffen, und die Rechtspflege durch Anordnung competenter Gerichte gesichert werden.

Art. 17. Bei Arbeiten, welche der Verein für eigene Rechnung ausführen lässt, wird er die Einwanderer vorzugsweise verwenden.

    Ein Beschluss der Direction wird dafür einen Preiss-Tarif festsetzen. Es wird der Lohn in Anweisungen auf die Empfänger lautend, ausbezahlt, emittirt in Gefolge des § 8 der Vereins Statuten.

    Die Casse der Colonial-Direction nimmt diese Anweisungen an Zahlungsstatt an; sie werden auf Verlangen des Inhabers gegen Tratten auf die Colonial-Casse auf 10 Tage Sicht ausgewechselt. Da diese Anweisungen einen Repräsentativ-Gehalt bilden, so werden deren niemals für einen 2/3 des Capitals der Waaren und des Zuchtviehes Werth emittirt werden.

III. Rechte und Pflichten der Colonisten.

Art. 18. Jeder Colonist verfügt selbständig und frei über seine Zeit und seine Arbeit.

Art. 19. Diejenigen, welche für den Verein zu arbeiten angenommen werden, verpflichten sich ihm zu einer Arbeit, deren Dauer durch die Colonial-Direction nach der Jahreszeit und der Art der Arbeit geregelt ist.

Art. 20. Alle Colonisten sind zur Aufrechthaltung der Ordnung und Sicherheit in der Colonie mitzuwirken verpflichtet.

    Eine besondere Vorschrift, entworfen von der Colonial-Direction nach dem Bedürfniss der Colonie, wird die Art dieser Mitwirkung festsetzen.

Art. 21. Die Constitution und die Gesetze von Texas reguliren Rechte und Pflichten der Einwanderer als Bürger der Republik.

Art. 22. Jeder Einwanderer ist verpflichtet, drei auf einander folgende Jahre auf dem ihm überwiesenen Landstrich zu verbleiben, daselbst eine Wohnung zu errichten und 15 Acres Landes zu bebauen und zu umzäunen. Die Kosten der Vermessung der den Colonisten bewilligten Ländereien, sind von denselben zu erstatten.

Art. 23. Ein Verbalprozess constatirt die Besitz-Einweisung in die bewilligten Ländereien zur Ergänzung des provisorischen Rechtstitels, wovon in Art. 5 oben die Rede ist. Drei Jahre nach dieser Besitz-Einweisung werden diese provisorischen Rechtstitel gegen einen definitiven Rechtstitel umgetauscht, welchen die texanische Regierung ertheilt.

Art. 24. Stossen die bewilligten Ländereien auf daran hinfliessende Gewässer so sind die Colonisten verpflichtet einen Durchgangs-Weg zu gestatten, dessen Breite der Ortsgebrauch bestimmt.

Ebenso sind sie verpflichtet, die zum Strassen- und Canal-Bau und zu anderen das allgemeine Beste anstrebenden Bauten erforderdliche Ländereien abzulassen.

Nach Umständen geschehen diese Abtretungen umsonst oder gegen Vergütung. *Umsonst* nämlich, wenn diese Arbeiten in den drei ersten Jahren nach der Besitz-Einweisung und auf nicht angebauten, oder nicht bebauten Ländereien unternommen werden; *gegen Vergütung,* wenn diese Arbeiten nach jenen drei ersten Jahren unternommen werden, oder wenn sie angebaute oder bebaute Ländereien begreifen.

Diese Abtretungen gegen Vergütung haben statt gegen gerechte und vorausgehende Schadloshaltung und gemäss den gesetzlichen Erfordernissen.

Art. 25. Die Veräusserung der bewilligte Ländereien durch die Einwanderer, kann—gemäss besonderer Uebereinkunft—nur erst nach Ablauf eines Zeitraumes von fünf Jahren, vom Tage der Besitz-Anweisung an gerechnet, Platz greifen.

Art. 26. Richterfüllung der vorbemerkten Bedingungen zieht den Verlust der Rechte der Colonisten auf die ihnen bewilligten Grundstücke und die darauf ruhenden Vortheile und Privilegien nach sich.

Art. 27. Einwanderer, welche aus der Colonie nach Europa zurückzukehren beabsichtigen sollten, werden stets Aufnahme auf den Fahrzeugen des Vereins finden; es werdn alsdann die Kosten der Rückfahrt nach demselben Massstabe berechnet wie jene der Hinreise.

Art. 28. Es werden diese Statuten—erforderlichen Falls—der texanischen Regierung zur Genehmigung vorgelegt werden.

Art. 29. Es wird die Colonial-Direction, die einzig und allein das Wohl ihrer Colonisten bei allen ihren Einrichtungen anstrebt, eine Wittwen- und Waisen-Versorgungs-Anstalt in's Leben rufen, sobald die Seelenzahl der Colonie einen voraussichtlich günstigen Erfolg garantirt. Sie wird bei deren Verwaltung die Colonisten selbst betheiligten.

Art. 30. Um den Verkehr des Colonisten mit dem Vaterlande und umgekehrt des letztern mit der Colonie nach Kräften zu erleichtern, wird die Direction ein Post-Sicherheits-Bureau organisiren. Sie wird sich zu diesem Ende mit der Post-Verwaltung der vereinigten Staaten in Neu-Orleans und mit einem angesehenen Handlungshause daselbst in Beziehung setzen.

Art. 31. Der Verein wird Vorrathshäuser einrichten, worin die Colonisten nach der Erndte ein gewisses unbedeutendes Quantum an Getreide einliefern, und voraus dann die Misserndten oder bei besondern Unglücksfällen, welche einzelne Familien trifft, die nöthigen Vorräthe, unentgeldlich verabfolgt werden.

APPENDIX D.

CONSTITUTION OF THE VEREIN.*

General Statut für die Colonial-Niederlassungen des Vereins.

ERSTES CAPITEL.

Verwaltung.

Art. 1. Die Ländereien, nach welchen der Verein die Einwanderung richtet, nehmen den Titel Colonial-Niederlassungen an.

Es wird die General-Versammlung den jeder derselben zu verleihenden Namen bestimmen.

Art. 2. Es werden diese Niederlassungen im Namen des Vereins verwaltet; jede hat eine besondere Verwaltung.

Es besteht die Direction jeder solchen Niederlassung: Direction jeder solchen Niederlassung:
1. Aus einem Director und
2. Aus einem Rathe von fünf Personen.

Alle werden von dem Comite der Directoren bestellt. Den Vorsitz im Directorial-Rathe hat der Director. Im Falle des Absterbens oder des Verhindertseins des Directors rückt der zum voraus durch das Comite der Directoren bestellte Vice-Director interimistisch an dessen Stelle.

Art. 3. Der Colonial-Rath wird zusammengesetzt:
1. Aus einem Seelsorger,
2. Aus einem Arzt,
3. Aus einem Civil-Ingenieur,
4. Aus einem Rechnungsführer, und
5. Aus dem Handels-Agenten des Vereins.

Art. 4. Es ist die Dauer der Functionen der Colonial-Agenten nicht bestimmt; das Comite der Directoren normirt die des Directors; sie kann—je nachdem es das Interesse des Vereins erheischt—abgekürzt oder verlängert werden.

* *Handbuch*, pp. 82-95.

Art. 5. Es sind die Gehalte des Directors und der Agenten entweder fixe oder proportionelle; Art und Betrag derselben setzt das Comite der Directoren fest.

Art. 6. Der Colonial-Director verwaltet allein die seiner Oberaufsicht anvertraute Niederlassung, ihm liegen alle Verwaltungshandlungen ob. Die Agenten und Angestellten der Niederlassung stehen unter dessen unmittelbarer Aufsicht, er setzt sie ab, ersetzt sie provisorisch, so wie auch im Falle einer Erledigung, sei es im Administrativ-Dienste, sei es in jenem der Direction, unter der Auflage diese Absetzungen und Ernennungen durch das Comite der Directoren bestätigen zu lassen.

Er ist verpflichtet den delegirten Director binnen drei Monaten davon in Kenntniss zu setzen.

Art. 7. Der Rechnungsführer verwaltet die Casse, überwacht den Vollzug der Befehle des Directors und contrasignirt alle Acte der Verwaltung. Er ist Secretair des Directorial-Rathes.

Art. 8. Er macht dem Directorial-Rath die Vorschläge und hat bei der Abstimmung darüber berathende Stimme.

Der Secretair des Directorial-Rathes führt ein Register über die Anträge, er bemerkt dabei die Verwerfung oder Annahme derselben.

Es führt überdies die Direction ein Tagebuch über ihre Arbeiten und Amtshandlungen.

Alle drei Monate wird ein summarischer Auszug aus dem Register der Anträge und aus dem Tagebuch der Directoren eingeschickt.

ZWEITES CAPITEL.

Fond-Inventarium.

Art. 9. Der jeder Colonial-Niederlassung bestimmte Fond wird durch die General-Versammlung des Vereins festgesetzt.

Es bestimmt der Jahres-Voranschlag der Ausgabe, verglichen mit jedem der muthmasslichen Einnahmen, die in die Colonial-Casse jeder Niederlassung einzuschieszende Summe.

Das Comite der Directoren bezeichnet diejenigen finanziellen Anstalten der vereinigten Staaten Nordamerikas, zu welchen die Colonial-Direction sich in Beziehung gesetzt hat.

Art. 10. Um den Verkehr der Ansiedler mit diesen Anstalten zu erleichtern, werden Anweisungen auf den Inhaber lautend geschaffen, gemäss § 8 der Statuten des Vereins. Es werden diese Anweisungen als gangbare Münze angesehen und als solche in den Vereins-Cassen angenommen oder gegen Tratten auf ein Monat Sicht auf die Centralle-Casse des Vereins in Europa, auf Verlangen des Inhabers umgetauscht.

Art. 11. Alle drei Monate lässt der Colonial-Director eine Aufnahme des Cassenbestandes so wohl, als der Ausgabe anfertigen und in jedem Jahre am 31. December werden alle Rechnungen abgeschlossen. Es wird zu derselben Epoche durch des Directors Fürsorge ein Inventarium über den Vermögenstand jeder Niederlassung aufgenommen.

Im Monat August jedes Jahres entwirft der Colonial-Director einen voranschlag über Einnahme und Ausgabe der seiner Oberaufsicht anvertrauten Niederlassungen für das folgende Jahr, um denselben der Genehmigung des Directorial-Comites vorzulegen.

Es werden alle diese Urkunden, jede zu ihrer Zeit, dem Comite der Directoren eingesandt.

DRITTES CAPITEL.

Anordnung der Arbeiten.

Art. 12. Unmittelbar nach seiner Ankunft an Ort und Stelle lässt der Director, falls dies nicht schon früher geschehen ist, den Plan der Ländereien aufnehmen, auf welchen die Colonial-Niederlassung zu gründen ist. Es werden diese Ländereien in Loose von 640 Acres eingetheilt; jedes Loos erhält eine Ordnungs-Nummer.

Dem Director liegt es ob, die tauglichste Stelle zur Anlegung einer Stadt und von Dörfern ausfindig zu machen, er besorgt die Verloosung der Bauplätze, nachdem er das Gutachten des Directorial-Comites eingeholt hat.

Er lässt Vertheidigungs-Anstalten aufführen, wie er solche zur Sicherheit der Ansiedler nöthig erachtet.

Art. 13. Es setzt sich der Director, Namens des Vereins in direkte Beziehung zu der Regierung und deren Agenten, bezüglich aller des Colonials-Interesse berührenden Einrichtungen.

VIERTES CAPITEL.

Einweisung der Einwander.

Art. 14. Bei Ankunft der Einwanderer am Landungsplatz werden dieselben unmittelbar der Colonial-Niederlassung zugewiesen; Waggons werden zur Verfügung der Frauen und Kinder gestellt und dienen zugleich zum Transport der Effecten der Einwanderer.

Die Direction wird Fürsorge tragen, vom Anlandungspunkte bis zur Colonie, für Ernährung der Ankömmlinge zu sorgen.

Art. 15. Um den Einwanderern Unterkunft während der Nacht zu verschaffen, werden Zelte aufgeschlagen, bis sie ihre Wohnungen beziehen können.

Art. 16. In der Colonial-Niederlassung angekommen wird jede Familie in den Besitz ihres Ländereien Looses eingewiesen; die Nummer der Reihenfolge in den Registern des Vereins, unter welcher er eingetragen worden ist, entspricht der Nummer des Looses, welches ihm gehört.

    Ein über diese Einweisung aufgenommener Verbalprozess constatirt die Besitz-Einweissung; es giebt derselbe Verbalprozess zugleich an, ob durch des Vereins Fürsorge auf das dem Einwanderer überwiesenen Loose Gebäulichkeiten aufgeführt sind.

Art. 17. So weit Zeit und Umstände es erlauben, lässt die Direction Gebäulichkeiten aufführen; es werden diese Gebäulichkeiten nach einem Maasstabe und in der Art ausgeführt, dass ihr Kostenbetrag nicht fl. 60 übersteigt.

Art. 18. Der Taglohn der Arbeiter, welche im Dienste des Vereins in dem Colonial-Niederlassungen verwendet werden, wird durch die Direction festgesetzt; es wird dieser Taglohn jede Woche in Anweisungen auf den Empfänger lautend, wovon Art. 10 spricht, oder durch Lieferungen bezahlt.

FUENFTES CAPITEL.
Beziehungen der Ansiedler zu der Direction.

Art. 19. Es verschafft die Direction jedem Ansiedler entweder ein fertig gebautes Haus oder die Materialien zur Aufführung eines solchen; sie giebt ihm die Mittel zur Umzäunung und Anbauung von 15 Acres Landes; so wie die zur landwirthschaftlichen Einrichtung erforderlichen Ochsen, Kühe und Pferde.

    Es werden alle diese Lieferungen jedem Ansiedler vorschussweise gemacht.

Art. 20. Jedem Ansiedler wird eine eigene Rechnung in den Registern der Colonial-Direction eröffnet, es werden ihm darin alle Vorschüsse zur Last geschrieben, welche ihm—sei es unter welcher Benennung es immer wolle—geleistet worden sind. Interessen für das erste Jahr werden ihm keine berechnet.

    Die Rückzahlung findet zur Erndtezeit statt oder auch früher, wenn es der Ansiedler so vorziehen sollte; es nimmt die Direction von dem Schuldner Felderzeugnisse nach dem laufenden Preise an Zahlungsstatt an.

Art. 21. Es haftet der Direction für diese Vorschüsse das Eigenthum der Schuldner.

SECHSTES CAPITEL.
Politischer Zustand der Ansiedlungen.

Art. 22. Es sind die Colonial-Niederlassungen so wohl als die Ansiedler den Gesetzen von Texas unterworfen.

Art. 23. Um den Vollzug dieser Gesetze sowohl, als die Unterdrückung von Verbrechen und Vergehen zu sichern, und um zugleich Anstände und Streitigkeiten, welche sich zwischen den Ansiedlern untereinander oder zwischen ihnen und dem Vereine erheben könnten, auszugleichen und zu schlichten, wird die Colonial-Direction bei der Regierung die Anstellung von Richtern, die Herstellung competenter Gerichte, Ernennung und Installation einer Local-Behörde, alles entnommen aus dem Personal der Ansiedlung selbst, beantragen.

Art. 24. Die Direction wird es sich angelegen sein lassen, regelmässige Civilstands-Register zu eröffnen, Geburts-, Trau- und Sterb-Register aufzulegen.

Art. 25. Es werden—im allgemeinen Interesse—alle männlichen Ansiedler vom 17. bis 50. Jahre eine Stadt-Miliz bilden, um für die Sicherheit von Personen und Eigenthum zu wachen.

Die Direction überwacht deren Organization den texanischen Gesetzten entsprechend.

Art. 26. Eine Zeitung für Handel und Ackerbau, wird—wenn erst die Bevölkerung zahlreich genug ist—alle allgemeinen und Sonder-Interessen der Niederlassung besprechen; sie wird die Ansiedler über ihre Pflichten als Ackerbauer und Bürger aufklären.

SIEBENTES CAPITEL.
Gemeinnützige Anstalten.

Art. 27. Der Verein—unter Fürsorge der Direction—wird öffentliche Anstalten in's Leben rufen, welche das Gemeinwohl bedingt.

Sie werden sich nach der Seelenzahl und dem Bedürfniss der Bevölkerung richten.

Art. 28. Es sind diese Anstalten namentlich:

1. Eine Kirche, in welcher der Simultan-Gottesdienst gefeiert wird, so lange die Bevölkerung nicht zahlreich genug ist, um die Kosten der verschiedenen Culten, zu denen sie zählt zu bestreiten.

    Es wird in dieser Beziehung ein Ordnungs-Statut entworfen von der Colonial-Direction, und bestätigt von der Regierung, die Bedingungen dieser Anordnung festsetzen.

2. Eine oder mehrere Freischulen, wo die Kinder beiderlei Geschlechts eine moralische und religiöse Ausbildung erhalten, es wird ihnen darin Unterricht ertheilt im Lesen, Schreiben, Rechnen, in der deutschen und englischen Sprache.

3. Eine Kranken-Verpflegungs-Anstalt, verbunden mit einer Apotheke. Kranke, die zur Aufnahme gemeldet werden, werden darin unentgeldlich aufgenommen und sollen dort alle mögliche Heil- und Linderungs-Mittel finden.

4. Das Haus der Colonial-Direction, wo der Colonial-Rath seinen Sitz haben wird, wo sich die Archive der Colonial-Niederlassungen und provisorisch das Civilstands-Bureau der Niederlassung befinden wird.

ACHTES CAPITEL.
Vorkehrungen den Handel betreffend.

Art. 29. Der Verein eröffnet, unter Leitung der Colonial-Direction, ein Magazin oder einen Bazar für alle Verbrauchs-Gegenstände und Arbeitsgeräthschaften, welche das tägliche Bedürfniss der Ansiedler erheischt.

Die Direction wird es sich streng angelegen sein lassen, dass ihre Magazine stets die zweckentsprechenden Vorräthe, wie solche das Bedürfniss der Bevölkerung mit sich bringt, darbieten.

Art. 30. Sie erzieht Vieh, um gute Racen herzustellen und den Ansiedlern den erforderlichen Viehstand zu verschaffen.

Die Preise von Waaren und Vieh werden stets im Einklang mit dem Curse des zunächst gelegenen Marktes gehalten werden.

Art. 31. Sie nimmt—sei es auf laufende Rechnung, sei es gegen Baarkauf und nach übereingekommenen Preise—alle Ackerbau- und industriellen Erzeugnisse der Ansiedler an.

Es werden die laufenden Rechnungen jedes Jahr nach der Erndte vorgestellt.

Art. 32. Die nach dem ersten Jahre des Aufenthaltes in der Niederlassung den Ansiedler gemachten Vorschüsse werden mit 5 Proc. verzinset.

Art. 33. Es bezieht die Colonial-Direction alle zum Bedürfnisse ihrer Niederlassungen erforderlichen Waaren entweder direkt aus Deutschland oder aus Amerika; ebenso befördert sie nach der oder jeder anderen Gegend die Ackerbau-Erzeugnisse, welche sie durch Tausch oder Kauf erworben hat.

NEUNTES CAPITEL.
Industrielle Anstalten.

Art. 34. Je nachdem es das Bedürfniss der Niederlassungen mit sich bringt, werden industrielle Anstalten in's Leben gerufen; es setzt die Direction den Wirkungskreis jeder derselben fest und legt dem Comite der Directoren den Plan und die Mittel zur Ausführung vor.

Jedenfalls wird jede Niederlassung besitzen:
Eine Fruchtmühle,
Eine Schneidemühle,
Eine Mühle, um die Baumwolle zu reinigen.

Art. 35. Die mit Leitung dieser Anstalten beauftragten Agenten und Angestellten, sind gemäss Art. 6 der Oberaufsicht des Directors unterworfen.

Art. 36. Wenn die Colonial-Direction, nachdem sie das Gutachten des Comites der Directoren eingeholt hat, Strassen und Canäle anlegt, Brücken baut und anders das Gemeinwohl anstrebende Verbesserungen vornimmt, so wird sie nach Art. 24 des Colonial-Statuts, rücksicht der Berechtigung der Ländereien richten.

ZEHNTES CAPITEL.
Verfügungen bezüglich der Ländereien.

Art. 37. Es werden des Vereins Ländereien in der Art eingetheilt; dass diejenigen, welche sie nicht umsonst verleiht, zwischen diejenigen zu liegen kommen, welche verliehen und in Anbau genommen sind.

Art. 38. Das Comite der Directoren, auf Vorschlag des Colonial-Directors, setzt den Preis der Ländereien und jenen der Bauplätze der Städte und Dörfer, die Art der Zahlung, die Bedingungen der Verkäufe und den Zeitpunkt, wann dieselbe beginnen sollen, fest.

Art. 39. Es finden die Verkäufe im Namen des Vereins durch den Colonial-Director statt, es werden die dessfälligen Urkunden durch den Rechnungsführer contrasignirt.

ELFTES CAPITEL.
Allgemeine Verfügungen.

Art. 40. Wenn der Verein mehrere Niederlassungen begründet hat, wird er einen General-Commissair bestellen und diesen mit der Controlle aller Niederlassungen und mit jener der Wirksamkeit jeder einzelnen beauftragen.

Art. 41. Es werden vorstehenden Bestimmungen alle nöthig erachtete Verbesserungen, nach Genehmigung des Comites der Directoren, hinzugefügt werden.

APPENDIX E.

PETITION OF COUNT CARL VON CASTELL TO THE DUKE OF NASSAU.
(A. D. No. St. M. 2674.)

Dem Herren Grafen Carl von Castell zu Mainz wird auf sein bei seiner Durchlaucht dem Herzog, eingereichtes Gesuch um Genehmigung der Bildung einer Gesellschaft, welche den Zweck hat, den in den Freistaat Texas einwandernden Deutschen Hülfe und Schutz zu gewähren, eröffnet, dass Seine Herzogliche Durchlaucht weder bei der Bildung dieser Gesellschaft noch bei deren Versammlung im Herzogthum etwas zu erinnern gefunden, und die Genehmigung deshalb gerne ertheilt haben.

Wiesbaden, den 3. Mai, 1844.
Herzoglich Nassauisches Staats Ministerium.
In Auftrag des Staats-Ministers der Ministerial Referendar: Geheimrath.
        unterz: Vollpracht.
        vrdt: Stein.

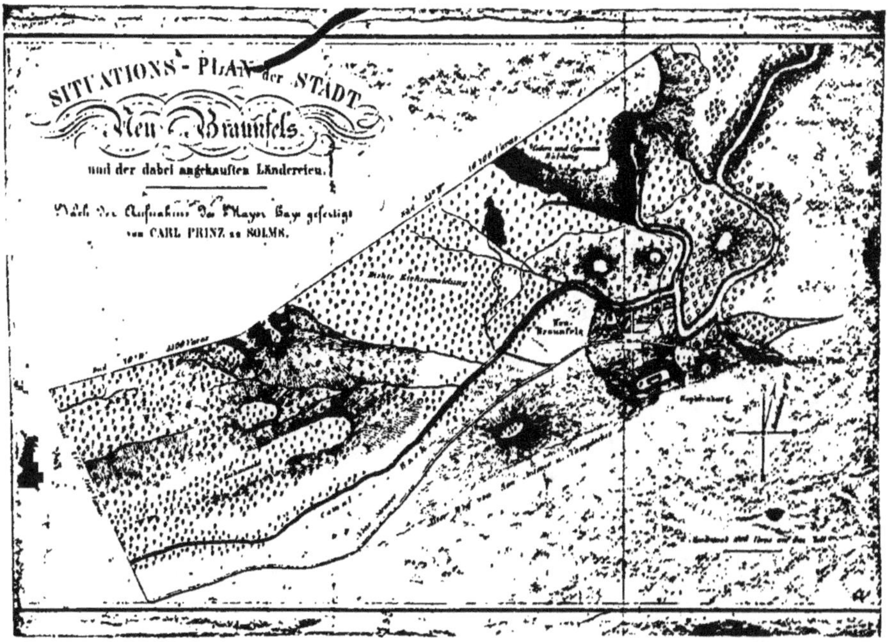

PLAN OF NEW BRAUNFELS IN 1846.

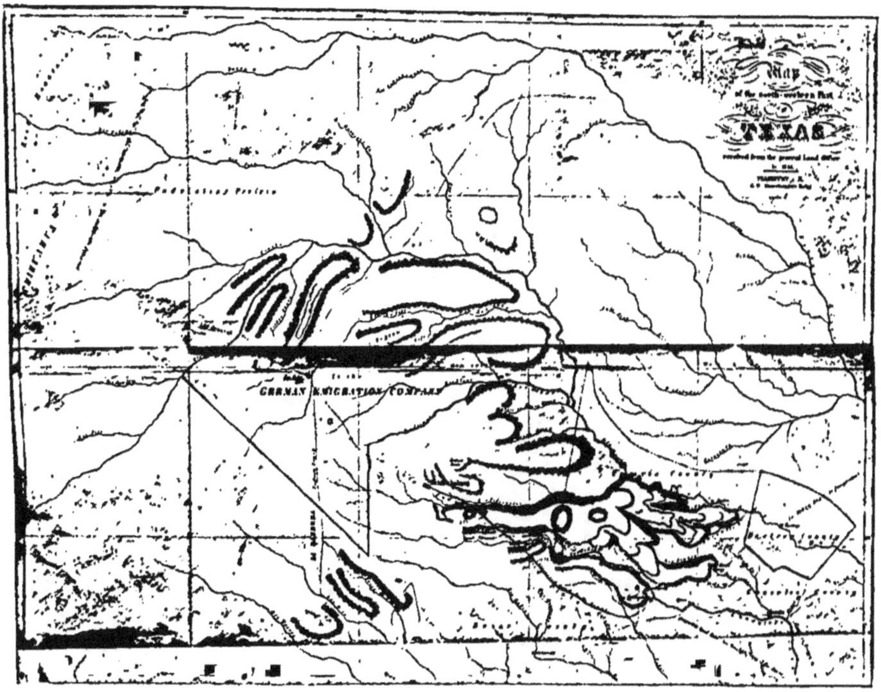

SITUATION OF THE GRANT IN 1846.

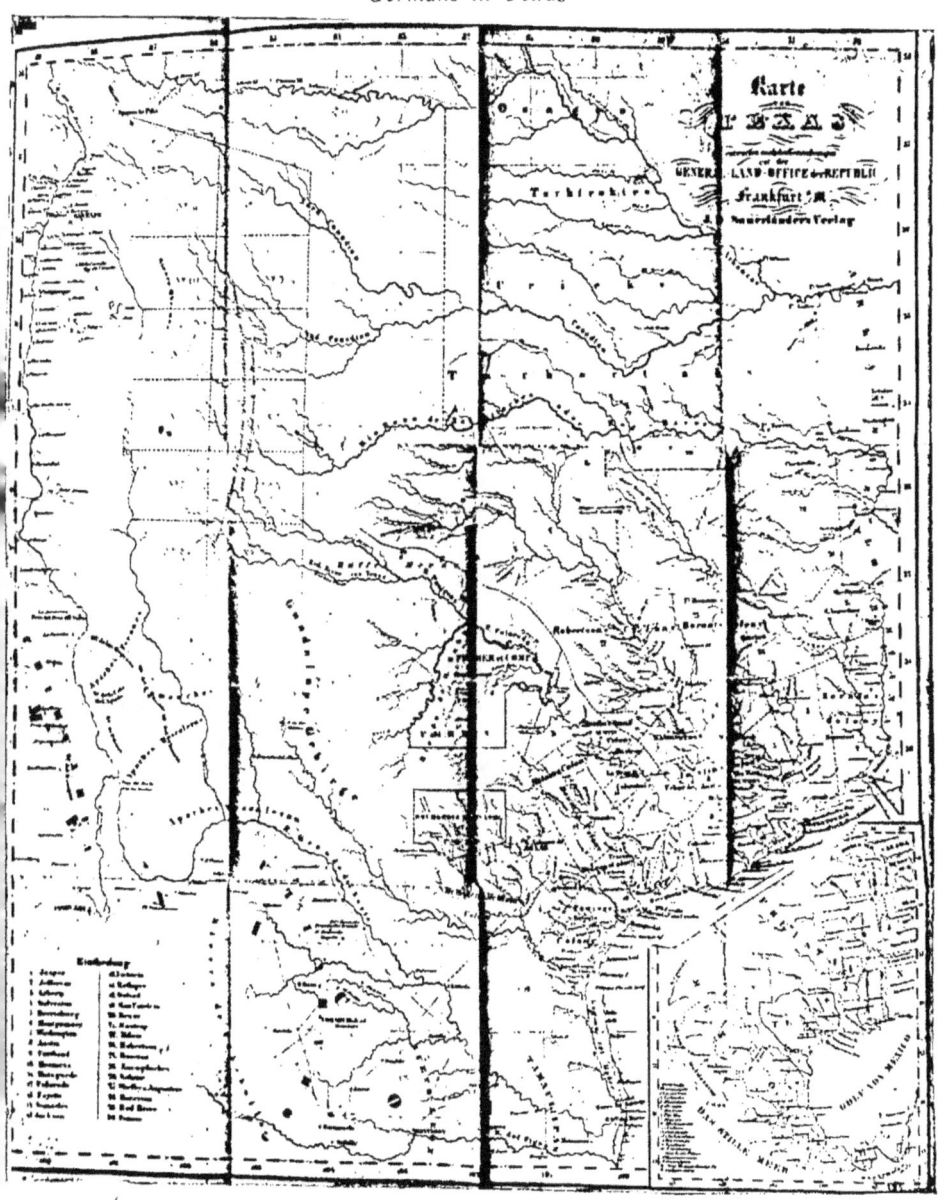

TEXAS IN 1846, SHOWING THE VEREIN GRANTS.

TEXAS IN 1848, SHOWING THE GERMAN SETTLEMENTS.

www.ingramcontent.com/pod-product-compliance
Lightning Source LLC
Chambersburg PA
CBHW052100230426
43662CB00036B/1715